Confessions of a Paris Potty Trainer

A HUMOROUS PARENTING MEMOIR

VICKI LESAGE

press

Published by Party Girl Press

ISBN-13: 978-1-4992-7653-4
ISBN-10: 1-4992-7653-2

Cover design by Ellen Meyer and Clara Vidal
Author photo by Mickaël Lesage and Damien Croisot

CATCH UP ON
Confessions

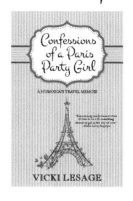

For Leonardo and Stella, who will always speak French better than me

Prologue

Confessions at the Check-Up

"OH LA LA," she said, surprised. "I can fit two fingers in there."

Quite a few situations spring to mind where this phrase might indicate good news. Un-wedging a child's stuck head from a banister. Retrieving a key through a sewer grate. Finger puppets.

A few are neutral. A kid learning he can pick his nose. Making yourself vomit, in case you ingested a poisonous substance. (That doesn't fit in the "good" category, lest I appear to support bulimia).

Most are bad. An exterminator discovering where the mouse that's been terrorizing your home originated from. Discovering a hole in the armpit of your shirt when you're running late for work. Realizing you got shorted two finger-widths of wine in the glass your hurried waitress dropped off before disappearing.

But when the French midwife said it to me at the end of my five-month pregnancy check-up, it was pretty much the worst news ever.

She extracted her gloved hand and calmly said, "You can get dressed now. Then we'll go to the ER."

I calmly replied, "Should I call my husband?"

She calmly responded, "Yes, that doesn't sound like a bad idea."

This was the last bit of calm we would have for a while.

Apparently, examining the cervix is routine in France but they don't do it in the U.S. or U.K. Pregnant women can walk around with dilated cervixes for months and not know it. I'm glad I knew, since I was subsequently placed on strict bed rest until Baby #2 arrived. Thanks, but I'd rather my baby not fall out on my way to the boulangerie. Who knew that nine years prior, when I first arrived in France, I would end up in stirrups, thankful a French woman had examined me with two fingers.

Not quite what I'd had in mind when I wanted to "immerse myself in the culture." But I was now a card-carrying member of the French health care system in all its probing and socialist glory.

I was drinking the Kool-Aid. What choice did I have? Alcohol was off-limits until Baby #2 arrived. This was going to be a long wait.

1

Safe Sex on the Beach

PERUSING THE CHALKBOARD MENU at the cozy Scottish pub, every drink looked good to me. Well, not the whisky. I don't need a drink that puts hair on my chest. I prefer something sweet. Or bubbly. Or both.

My husband, Mika, and I were seated at our usual spot at the bar. Mika had already ordered a beer. And our friend Anne Marie, the cheery Irish bartender with a wave of reddish hair, was giving me the eye.

"C'mon you. What's the big decision? Glass of wine like usual, yeah?"

A glass of Bordeaux isn't typical fare for a Scottish pub, except this particular bar was located in the Marais, a trendy but lovely part of Paris. Too trendy (read: expensive) for us to live in, so we lived in the less trendy (read: still expensive but at least doable) 15th *arrondissement*.

Mika and I were frequent customers of this bar, partly because we loved it and partly because Anne Marie now worked there. She'd previously been employed at the posh

Swedish Society, the private club where we'd been regulars and also where we had our wedding reception.

Now just a few short months after I'd entered into marital bliss, I was pregnant with my first baby.

Hence the drink dilemma.

I've read numerous articles about French doctors being pretty lenient concerning drinking while pregnant, saying that as long as you limit it to one glass of red wine per day, it's not a big deal. However, *my* doctor didn't say that. I'm beginning to think it's an urban legend, propagated to make the French seem loose and carefree and make Americans jealous.

Articles and stereotypes aside, I had already decided I wouldn't drink during my pregnancy. Which, as a well-known party girl, was going to be difficult.

In my pre-pregnant days—in an effort to make sure my perfect-for-jeans butt still fit in said jeans even after consuming vast amounts of champagne and wine and shots and... I'll stop there since my mom is going to read this—I had formed a policy. I only allowed myself to consume caloric beverages if they contained alcohol. This meant that water, black coffee, and diet soda were OK. But no juice or non-diet soda or energy drinks or any of those other empty calorie explosions.

However, when faced with a bar menu, the only choices without alcohol have calories. Might be time to revise my policy. I was eating for two now, right? I could handle the extra calories.

The other part of the dilemma was that I hadn't told Ammo yet that I was pregnant. I had just reached the 12th week and Mika and I had jointly decided it was now safe to share the news. Our parents already knew but no one else. A Facebook post would be the easiest way to reach my friends in all corners of the world (have we really not modified that expression since we discovered the earth was round?). But then the friends I normally saw in person might be offended that's how they found out. But then again, with the fatigue of pregnancy already setting in, combined with the fact that I couldn't drink, I wasn't making the rounds with my friends as often as I used to.

And holy smokes, how long had I been sitting here thinking about this while Anne Marie was waiting for an answer?

If I wasn't careful I would turn into one of the annoying French customers who comes to a pub, takes forever to order, settles on the cheapest option, then nurses their drink all night while watching the game on TV. I wouldn't be allowed to make fun of those people if I was doing the exact same thing.

"Um, what's good that doesn't have alcohol? My stomach feels a bit…"

"OH. MY. GOD. Vicki Lesage is pregnant. Oh my god! Congratulations you two!" Anne Marie bounded out from behind the bar and embraced us in a bear hug.

I could have tried to deny it, but I had been planning on telling her anyway. "How did you know?"

"Um, when have you ever not ordered alcohol in a bar? If you were sick you would have stayed home." She had a point. "Wow. Congrats."

"Thanks," Mika chimed in, his big brown eyes creasing at the corners as he couldn't help but smile.

"I have to ask, you know, since you just got married. Accident or planned?"

I would have been shocked except Ammo always asked questions like this. "You know how organized I am! Of course this wasn't on accident, it was planned down to the minute."

"I shoulda known. And I see you're still saying 'on accident.'"

She'd corrected me several times before, to no avail. "Sorry, but 'by accident' just doesn't sound right. You either do something on purpose or on accident. You wouldn't say you did something 'by purpose.'"

Mika continued sipping his beer, glancing at the game. The subtleties of the English language were lost on my French husband. Then again, apparently they were lost on me, too.

"Anyway, your drink. Without alcohol. Are you sure you're going to be OK? Nine months without alcohol?"

"Well, I'm already three months in, so we're a third of the way there. It's rough but it's for a good cause."

"Yeah, yeah. OK, how about I make you a Safe Sex on the Beach?"

"So, a juice?" That didn't fit my no-calorie policy and it sounded terribly boring.

"It's not a juice if you call it Safe Sex on the Beach. This is as much fun as you'll be having for a while, so try to enjoy it." She winked before turning around to mix up my concoction.

As I waited for my "cocktail," I sized up the situation. I had taken forever to order, I ended up with the cheapest drink on the menu, and was probably going to nurse it all night since there's no point in chugging juice. The only thing keeping me from being a fully annoying French customer was the fact I wasn't watching the game. Oh, and the fact that I was American. But with a French husband and a half-French baby on the way, I was dangerously close.

After a few splashes from various juice bottles and vigorous shakes with a martini shaker (ah, martinis), Ammo poured my Safe Sex on the Beach into an ice-filled glass. Then she poured a shot of whisky[1] for herself.

---

[1] American and Irish readers might be thinking "Um, isn't it spelled 'whiskey'?" The answer is: yes and no. Some countries who produce the liquor spell it with an 'e,' some don't. The easiest way to remember is that countries that produce it whose name contains an 'e,' such as The United States and Ireland, spell it with an 'e.' Countries that produce it whose name does not contain an 'e,' such as Scotland,

"Cheers to my old, married, knocked-up friend. Congrats."

Ammo, Mika, and I clinked glasses.

"Cheers."

Canada, and Japan, spell it without the 'e.' As an American in France talking about the liquor being served in a Scottish pub, I could probably get away with either spelling, but decided to go with the Scottish way since Ammo was drinking Scotch whisky. Whew! After all that, I might need a shot of whisky after all.

2

Leave Your Modesty at the Border

AMERICANS ARE KNOWN FOR BEING PRUDES, and I'm no exception. I may party (or rather, *used* to, sigh) with the best of them but when it comes to getting naked, I'm as Puritan as they come.

When Mika surprised me, just three months after we started dating, with a trip to Iceland for my birthday, I was ecstatic.

"Blue Lagoon, here I come!" I'd said.

"Can't wait. And did you know they let you drink beer in the lagoon?" This man knew the way to my heart.

"No I didn't! How cool is that? Thank you," I'd said, standing on my tiptoes to kiss my tall, dark, and handsome boyfriend. "This is literally the best present ever."

Sure enough, once we'd arrived at the famed lagoon, I peered out the window of the visitor's lodge and saw people relaxing along the edges of the sky blue water, sipping lager. While your body is enjoying the 100-degree temperature of the lagoon (that's 38 degrees Celsius to the rest of the world), the frigid Icelandic air keeps your beer cool. This place was made for me.

But before I could dive in, I had to make a mandatory stop at the public showers. Yuck. First, you changed into your swimsuit in a sauna-like locker room. I survived this portion by changing in the restroom, but that only provided a temporary reprieve. Numerous signs indicated "All swimmers MUST shower before entering the lagoon. This means you, Vicki."

Women stripped out of their swimsuits, showered in the door-free stalls, redressed, then exited as if this wasn't the most horrifying experience of their lives.

I froze in panic.

Did I really have to strip down in front of all these people? I couldn't see a way around it—if I walked out with dry hair everyone would know I'd broken the rules. And, at heart, I'm someone who follows the rules.

"Afsakið," a blonde, elderly woman said as her naked body brushed past me. I was pretty sure that meant "excuse me," from the smattering of Icelandic phrases I'd researched before the trip.

What I was worried about? The room was a sea of wrinkles and sags that my 29-year-old body had not yet fallen victim to, plus my Nordic shower companions weren't even looking in my direction. In fact, I was the only one staring at everyone's nakedness.

I was the locker room perv.

And, oddly, the sole way to remedy the situation was to remove my clothes.

I dashed to the corner stall, despite the "No Running, You Prudish American" sign and cranked on the spray. Fortunately it was instantly hot—the showers in Iceland are heated by thermal gas, which smells like rotten eggs but I weirdly like it—so I was able to get in and out and back into my suit before anyone could wonder "Who's that pale weirdo in the corner?"

As I pushed open the wooden door, the cool air punched me in the face. Damn, that was cold.

"Here you go honey," Mika said, handing me a beer.

How did he have time to shower *and* buy beers? Oh yeah, as a Frenchman he probably just stripped down and hosed off like the rest of the Europeans without giving it a second thought. Why was I so uptight? It was getting in the way of my drinking!

"Thanks," I said, taking a sip. "Ready? Let's get our buns in the water before we freeze."

☙❧

Now, three short years later, I was used to the relaxed European attitude toward nudity, if still not entirely comfortable with it. Which came in handy for the slew of doctor's appointments scheduled throughout my pregnancy.

Standard French practice during *grossesse*[2] is to visit a gynecologist for the first three monthly check-ups, then the rest of the check-ups are handled by a *sage-femme* (midwife) at the hospital where you registered to deliver.

My first few appointments were with Docteur Grandier. Like many doctors I'd visited before, his office was a converted apartment. The waiting room was much like a typical French living room, with ancient hardwood floors, crisp white walls, and elegant crown molding.

"Bonjour, Madame Lesage," he said, extending a bear paw in greeting. He shook Mika's hand as well, then led us

---

[2] "Grossesse" means "pregnancy" in French, but doesn't it look much more accusatory than that? The obvious insult is the "gross" part, like "Ew, gross, look how flabby she's getting." But taking it a step further, the French word for fat is "gros," or "grosse" if you're referring to a female. So, they really *are* saying I'm fat! Trying to throw a little "esse" on the end doesn't make it look nicer – I will forever be hung up on the "gross" bit.

back to his office, which doubled as the exam room. It must have been a bedroom back when the apartment was an actual apartment, but now it had an examination table instead of a bed, and a neatly-kept desk in one corner.

Mika and I sat down in two plush armchairs in front of the desk while Docteur Grandier rattled off questions, writing the answers by hand on a piece of notebook paper. The creation of my maternity *dossier*. The French and their dossiers! And their love for handwriting when they could just as well be typing and printing it out!

"Now I will do the examination," he said in French, waving an arm to indicate the table and stirrups waiting for me on the other side of the room. I looked over at the table and back at the doctor. This was going to be uncomfortable.

At my gynecologist's office in my hometown of St. Louis, Dr. Branson handles things a bit differently. And from what I've gathered from other Americans, his way is how everyone in the U.S. does it. A nurse leads you to the room, they give you a flimsy paper sheet to cover up with, they leave you to undress from the waist down and lamely try to cover up with said sheet, then you wait for the doctor. He does the exam and asks if you have any questions, all with a disposable sheet between him and your business. Then he leaves, you get dressed, and, because he shares an office with a pediatrician, you snag a lollipop on the way out.

But Docteur Grandier's posh Parisian office had no nurses and no disposable sheets. Not even a lollipop to distract me.

From my accent it was obvious I was American, so he graciously construed my hesitation as miscomprehension. In English he said, "You may undress and go to the exam table."

Now I had no excuse. Well, if I was going to be a mother soon, I might as well learn how to act like an adult.

I stood up, undressed in front of my husband and doctor, and marched my naked booty over to the luxurious table.

The consultation went fine and I even had a nice surprise at the end—we got to see our baby on an ultrasound monitor! I had been so thrown off by the fact that we seemed to be in someone's apartment that it hadn't occurred to me he would have such a snazzy machine.

At that point I was only five weeks along so the image was more blob than baby but it was my little blob. I squinted and rotated the print-out 90 degrees. Still a blob.

Well, who cared if I was looking at it right, Baby Blob was adorable to me.

3

You Mean French Efficiency *Isn't* an Oxymoron?

AFTER TWO MORE CHECK-UPS with Docteur Grandier, I transferred to L'Hopital Armand Trousseau. Mika and I had debated on whether to register at a private or public hospital, but had heard such good things about Trousseau (a public hospital) that we decided to take our chances there.

Maybe I'd have to share a room or the hospital would be gross or maybe it would be totally fine. My experience with the French health care system had been positive thus far, so I figured it would be OK. Plus, it was close to Mika's parents' house, which could come in handy.

The hospital didn't disappoint. From a purely superficial standpoint, it was gorgeous. The original brick buildings dated from the early 1900's and centered around a flowery square with park benches. A more modern structure towered behind these classic buildings, and it was in this part of the hospital that most of the activity took place. I found it to be the best of both worlds—it's charming to pass such lovely architecture but at the same time, I felt much more comfortable being cared for in a high-tech building.

The hospital staff surprised me with their efficiency and courtesy, two qualities I hadn't thought the French had a translation for. They even sent text messages with appointment reminders!

Of course, that didn't stop them from hand writing everything in my dossier.

Mika and I arrived for my first appointment with a large folder from Docteur Grandier's office that included his scrawled notes, blood test results, a stack of legal and official documents, and Baby Blob's adorable photo.

First stop—complete my registration. After years of prolonged paperwork for my tourist visa, work visa, and marriage certificate, I was apprehensive. Would they send me home to fetch item #11 on the 10-point list? Would they hassle me because one of my documents wasn't quite right? Would I even understand what they were saying?

"Bonjour, Madame et Monsieur Lesage. Why don't you go ahead and take yourself a seat, dearies?" The smiling, dark-skinned lady behind the desk had the same boisterous manner many African-American nurses had back in the U.S. "How you feeling, honey? Good? Good. Now you just let me work through my files and I'll get you on to the next step in no time." She hummed a jaunty tune as she shuffled the mound of papers.

Spacing out in the comfortable chairs in front of her desk, minutes or hours could have passed and I wouldn't have known. I was relaxed and no one was harassing me with questions I couldn't answer or files I couldn't produce. Pretty much the exact opposite of every other administrative encounter I'd had in France.

Once the papers had been shuffled the requisite number of times, the nurse showed us down the hall to the urine analysis station. Mika sat off to the side while I stood in line with the other ladies and stared at their bumps trying to guess how far along they were without getting caught.

I also scoped out their maternity wear. Clad in my usual jeans, shirt, and knee-high boots ensemble, I felt pretty good about my appearance. Only four months along, I didn't appear pregnant to the casual observer.

But compared to the French ladies, I was frumpy. Even with a watermelon protruding from their bellies, these women, dressed head-to-toe in black with a scarf artfully draped around the neck, were the epitome of fashion.

And they were all so petite! At 5'6" (167 centimeters to those who think a cat jumped on my keyboard) and 140 pounds (64 kilos), I wasn't huge and wasn't small. But here I felt about double the size of everyone else.

The bathroom door opened and out came another one of these petite wonders. Well, she still had to hold a cup of pee, no matter how svelte she was. That made me feel better.

Once I had my own cup of embarrassment in hand, I scurried down the brightly lit hallway to the nurse's station to drop it off for analyzing.

"Hop on the scale, honey," a thin, gorgeous black nurse instructed.

I did as I was told and was shocked when I saw 68 kilos.

"How much does the scale say, honey?" she said, dipping a testing stick into my cup.

"Um, 68 kilos but I have boots and jeans on, so you know…"

"Don't worry, sweetie, I'll deduct for the boots." She jotted a number on my urine results ticket, then escorted Mika and me down a different hall to wait for the next part of the appointment.

As soon as she left, I checked the slip of paper to see how much she'd deducted. Half a kilo. That's all? Some quick math told me that was slightly over a pound. Hrm. I'd have to weigh my jeans and boots when I got home. And maybe next time wear a sundress and sandals, even though we were experiencing one of the coldest winters Paris had seen in years.

I know it's not a competition, but it's hard to watch the scale creep up to numbers you've never seen before while everyone else in the waiting room is the size of your pinky finger.

"Madame Lesage?" A young *sage-femme* with long, brown, wavy hair peeked her head around the corner and smiled. "Follow me."

Even the midwives were gorgeous! In fact, I was pretty sure I hadn't seen one average-looking person since I arrived. How could that be? Did the public hospital double as a modeling agency? Or was that the norm in France?

I held Mika's hand as I padded down yet another hallway, self-conscious about my jiggling flab and imagining my footsteps sounded like a herd of elephants. I really needed to get over this since I was only going to get bigger!

The *sage-femme's* office was similar to Docteur Grandier's in that it had a desk with two chairs and everyone's favorite exam-table-with-stirrups. And no curtain or paper sheet. At least I was used to it by now.

The *sage-femme* heaved open my dossier and fired off questions, dutifully noting my responses (by hand, of course) on the bright yellow sheet of paper.

"Est-ce que vous avez des allergies?"

"Des problèmes pulmonaires?"

"Des problèmes cardiaque? Hypertension?"

"Avez-vous déjà été opérée?"

Who knew I understood so much French? It helped that many words were similar to English but with a cuter accent. And responding was easy when every answer was "No."

"Fumez-vous?"

No, of course I didn't smoke.

"Buvez?"

Did I drink? "Before I was pregnant? Lots." I chuckled. Mika rolled his eyes. The *sage-femme* stared, unsmiling. "But since I've been pregnant, no."

She checked a box and moved on to the next question. Why did I have to make a joke? Now she probably hated me and thought I would be a horrible mom.

"Avez-vous déjà fait une dépression nerveuse?"

What? Crap, I totally missed what she said. I turned to Mika and mouthed "What?" while trying not to panic.

"Have you ever had a nervous breakdown," he clarified.

I stifled the urge to make another stupid joke and say "Right now!" and instead smartly responded with "No." I'd get through this like a responsible adult if it killed me.

After eleventy billion more questions, it was exam time.

"You can undress from the waist down and I'll meet you over there," the *sage-femme* instructed. "I have one more form to fill out."

I did as I was told. I'd prove to her how mature I could be!

She began by listening to the baby's heartbeat, which was awesome. Whoomp, whoomp, whoomp, twice as fast as an adult heartbeat.

Next up: blood pressure, which I'm always overly proud of. My family on my dad's side are walking heart attacks while my mom's blood pressure is slightly above that of a corpse. They usually have to take her blood pressure a few times just to be sure she's still alive.

Mine is normally around 100 over 60, or as they say in France, 10 over 6. What an odd thing to do differently.

"Ten over six," she said, as I beamed at my husband. He obligingly smiled back, ever supportive of even the tiniest accomplishments.

Just then someone knocked at the door. "Oui?" the *sage-femme* called.

"Hello, I'm here to watch." A statuesque blonde supermodel with *Sage-Femme, Étudiante* emblazoned on her badge entered the room.

"Yes, of course. Madame Lesage, I forgot to tell you there would be a student stopping by. Is that OK with you?"

Let's see. I was already spread eagle on the exam table with my husband and the *sage-femme* talking to what I wish was my face but wasn't. Why not invite someone else to the party?

"Pas de problème," I answered.

I turned my head and focused on the wall across the room adorned with birth announcements. I squinted to read the baby names, seeing if any names sounded better to me than the ones Mika and I had already discussed.

"All done! Everything looks good."

I gave Mika my characteristic proud look and he returned his usual supportive smile. If they had greeting cards that said "Your cervix is doing a great job," he surely would have sent me one.

"Bonne journée," we said to the *sage-femmes* as we exited the room.

Walking down the corridor, hand in hand with my husband, I couldn't have been happier. With the exam behind me, and only good news to report, I had a spring in my step. So what if I was chubbier than French women? My baby was healthy and my husband worshipped the ground I waddled on.

Life was good.

4

Pack It Up, Pack It In, Let Me Begin. Again.

BY THE TIME SPRING ROLLED AROUND, we decided to move. Well, not so much decided as were told by our landlords, "We want our apartment back so we can combine it with the apartment next door and have a super nice place while you're forced to live on the street."

They were obligated to honor our lease and let us stay until December, but offered us the incentive of a free month's rent if we were out by June. Given how exorbitant our rent was, I was determined to take them up on this offer. Not to mention that our baby was due in September so it would be way easier to move now than at the end of the year when we would have a baby and loads of baby stuff to move as well.

Apartment searches in Paris are about as fun as having a tooth pulled. And I should know. I've had 13 teeth pulled (my baby teeth would not fall out!) and, at that point, six apartments in Paris.

Before even starting your search, you have to compile your dossier. If you show up to visit an apartment without one, they will laugh you out the door and promptly accept the dossier of one of the other twenty people who showed up prepared.

You need rent receipts from your current place (you're screwed if you're hunting for your first apartment), paystubs, bank statements, DNA samples, and letters from your mom attesting to your good behavior.

Then you need to schedule one of the sought-after viewings and show up early, only to find that people more desperate than you arrived an hour ago.

When the douchebag real estate agent (they always are) opens the door, a stampede ensues while everyone thrusts their dossier in his arms, then scopes out the place they just begged to pay upwards of €1,500 a month for.

"I guess we could strip the wallpaper."

"I could probably cook dinner standing sideways."

"The dog urine smell will eventually go away."

Yet you still stand there like a loser, hoping Douchebag picks you.

"We will contact you if you're selected," he says with an apathetic sigh. "Does anyone need a last look or can I lock up?"

You've seen as much of this dump as you can handle, so you walk out, hopes high but head hung low. It's a lose-lose situation. If you do get picked, you'll have to live here. If you don't get picked, you'll have to go through this process all over again, potentially ending up someplace worse.

Needless to say, we weren't thrilled with having to look for an apartment. At least this time our dossier was thicker than on previous expeditions. We were now married, which reassures landlords that you won't break up and therefore makes them more likely to rent to you (have they seen recent divorce statistics?). Sucks for singles but we needed every leg up we could get!

Also, I now had paystubs, as I'd taken a job at a French company a year earlier. Previously, landlords didn't know what to think of my American freelance income, even though I had earned double what I was now making in France. You want paystubs, Douchebag? Come and get 'em! I chopped down five trees just to prove I work in this country!

After packing our dossier full of as much information as we thought necessary (and then some), we visited a few apartments in our neighborhood.

Each one was a bust.

The first apartment didn't have a single right angle. Furniture was pushed awkwardly against the walls, leaving little walking room. We submitted our dossier anyway, but an engineering student (which I know because she said it 42 times) with rich parents had slipped her dossier in before ours. I don't know how you get paystubs as a student but I guess rich parents trump working for your money. Fine, she could have her odd-shaped apartment.

The agent for the second place must have owned the world's best camera because the ad showed expansive rooms where I had already mentally arranged our furniture. When we showed up, I nearly got stuck in the kitchen. Certainly in a few months my pregnant belly would be so big that I wouldn't be able to turn around in it. I would literally have to back out and re-enter at a different angle. We submitted our dossier anyway, but a slightly older and better dressed couple sauntered in after us and since they didn't get stuck in the kitchen, I'm assuming they're the ones who got the apartment.

Not entirely dejected yet, we tried one more apartment. It was situated on the second floor of a classic stone Parisian building and adjacent to my favorite *boulangerie*. Perfect. The courtyard overflowed with blossoming trees and French music played in the distance, likely emanating from someone's open window, adding to the charm. I had to have this apartment!

An elegant, regal woman opened the door, revealing the most bizarre foyer I'd ever seen.

Let me take that back. I did NOT have to have this apartment. But we politely (and desperately) decided to have a look anyway.

The front door opened directly on to a half flight of stairs. That's weird enough—like, who wants to go up more stairs right when they walk in—but these steps were carpeted. And the worn carpet was coral colored. My senses had been brutally assaulted and I hadn't even crossed the threshold.

We mounted the stairs and were met with a whole reef of coral carpet in the living room.

"You'll notice the double-paned windows and numerous built-in closets," the agent purred.

Um, no I won't! I was still blinded from the carpet.

"It could be worse," Mika whispered.

"Is that the bar we've set for ourselves? That as long as it could be worse we'll take it?"

"The kitchen is decent, at least."

I glanced over at the newly redone kitchen. He was right. OK, maybe we could do this. Maybe once the furniture was in place the carpet wouldn't be so noticeable. And it's not that I was against stairs—hey, free exercise— it's just that once the baby came I wasn't sure I wanted a staircase *in* our apartment. But many people lived in houses with stairs and did just fine. And if the kitchen was this nice, maybe the bathroom had been renovated as well.

Wait a minute, where *was* the bathroom? We hadn't come across it yet, but the apartment wasn't exactly huge. Where could it be hiding?

I've heard horror stories from friends in Paris about apartments where the bathroom was in the hallway of the building, shared by all residents on the floor. I've also heard of tenants having to use their landlord's bathroom, their own "apartment" actually just being a weirdly partitioned series of rooms previously attached to the landlord's dwelling.

For the price this lady was asking, that better not be the situation here.

"Pardon, mais, où sont les toilettes?" I asked the agent.

She'd been gazing out the window but quickly turned around with a smile. "Oh yes! You haven't seen it yet. It's been recently updated like the kitchen. Follow me."

Maybe this wouldn't be so bad.

We headed toward the staircase and the front door. Uh oh. Maybe this *would* be bad.

She marched down two steps, then unlatched a door that was recessed into the wall and hovered over three of the steps.

OK, where the heck did that come from? I hadn't noticed that door when we first arrived, probably because the carpet had been busy burning holes in my corneas.

She extended her arm to indicate we could enter, while she remained firmly planted on the steps. In a clumsy gymnastic move, I hopped from the second step into the bathroom. I had to admit, once you leapt inside, it wasn't bad.

Fresh sunlight streamed through the translucent window and the room was quite sizeable for a Parisian apartment.

I looked back to Mika at the top of the stairs. While his legs were much longer than mine and could probably bridge the gap more easily, he was clumsier than me. He's like a puppy—sweet, loving, and always knocking stuff over.

"Are you coming in?" I asked.

"No, I can see it from here."

I exited the bathroom with as much grace as I could manage and stood next to Mika on the steps as the agent edged away to give us some privacy.

"Should we submit our dossier?" he whispered.

"Between the carpet and the stairs and the acrobatic maneuvers necessary to enter the bathroom, I'm not sure I'm into this place."

"Me neither, but we're running out of options."

I shrugged my shoulders. "We might as well try. We'll probably get rejected anyway."

Mika turned back to the agent and handed her our dossier. "We're concerned about the stairs and the access to the bathroom, but I guess we'll figure it out."

"Oh really?" She seemed genuinely surprised that we didn't want to pole vault into the bathroom. "I've never heard anyone mention that before."

She couldn't be serious. Were we being too picky? Or was she just weird?

She flipped through our dossier, then slid it into her briefcase. "I'll review your file in my office and will let you know by tomorrow if you've been selected."

There was competition for this place? Unreal.

"Merci, Madame. À bientôt," Mika said as he ushered me out the door.

§∞∞§

"Would you like some champagne, Vicki?" Mika's dad, Gilbert, asked.

"Gilbert! What are you thinking?" Catherine, Mika's mom, lightly slapped him on the forearm.

"Oops, I'm sorry, I forgot." Though Gilbert had blue eyes and sandy blond hair, he looked just like Mika with his sheepish expression.

We were at Mika's parents' house for our ritual Sunday lunch. Normally we indulged in bubbly and wine and then more bubbly with dessert. It's no wonder I got along with his amiable parents so well.

And even though they were excited about the impending birth of their first grandchild, they still hadn't gotten used to their daughter-in-law not drinking. I had quite the reputation.

"No problem!" I said. "I'll just have some sparkling water in a champagne flute." A girl could pretend.

"So I guess we didn't get that last apartment," Mika said.

"We didn't want that coral piece of crap anyway. When the baby is born and I'm done nursing, I'm going to drink like nobody's business. And if we lived in that booby trap, I would fall down those stairs on my way for a late night bathroom visit. No thanks."

"I know we didn't want it but it still hurts to be rejected."

"Have you guys considered the 12th?" Gilbert suggested.

Catherine's dark eyes lit up. "Yes! You could live near us! For the same size apartment it's a bit cheaper here, so maybe it would be easier to get your dossier accepted. Let's have a look," she said, walking over to her computer.

Before I knew it, we had viewed a plethora of online listings for the 12th *arrondissement*. The apartments were still expensive—nowhere in Paris is cheap—but they were a smidge more affordable than what we'd seen in the 15th.

I'd lived in the 15th the entire time I'd been in Paris (seven years!) and it seemed scary to move. Then again, it would be nice to live close to Mika's parents.

"It can't hurt to look," I said.

We raised our glasses and toasted. "To the 12th!"

5

Hunting for a Treasure

ONCE WE DECIDED to look for an apartment in the 12th *arrondissement*, the search became much easier. At least for me. That's because, since Mika had grown up in the neighborhood, I let him do all the searching. I'll wait while you nominate me for Wife of the Year.

While Mika was running around on his lunch breaks and in the evenings, checking out potential apartments, I was busy baking our little bun in the oven. Fair trade, right?

"I found the one," Mika said over the crackling cell phone line.

"I sure hope you're talking about apartments and not a new wife."

"Very funny. Can you check it out tonight just to be sure? I saw it at lunch and think it's great, but you know better than me."

So true. He hadn't even minded the coral carpet so I definitely needed to have a look-see before we signed the lease.

That night, we swung by the apartment on our way home from work. Amazingly, even though I had to cross to the other side of town, it took the same amount of time to get there from my office. It was a straight shot on Métro Line 1 and I could zone out reading a book instead of having to transfer lines. Nice.

"Hi honey," I said, kissing Mika as we met on the sidewalk in front of the building. "The guy's not here yet?"

"Nope. But at lunch he didn't seem that douchey so hopefully he won't make us wait."

A scooter engine puttered behind us and came to a stop. A young, attractive guy hopped off, removed his helmet, then came over to shake hands. He was well dressed, with some seriously luscious locks of dark hair. He had all the makings of a douche but somehow just wasn't.

"Your dossier is already approved," Luscious Locks informed us as he punched in the door code.

The apple red door opened onto a quaint cobbled courtyard. Flowers bloomed in pots lining the building, while several large trees filled the center square.

The apartment was on the first floor (so, up one flight of stairs according to the French way of counting floors) with a view overlooking the courtyard. Glancing quickly around the place, I was sold.

I'd already seen the listing online and the price, size, and location were perfect. I'd just needed to see for myself that the bathroom wasn't hanging off the edge of a cliff or that the floor didn't secretly host shag carpeting. My minimal criteria were met.

"We'll take it!" I shouted.

෴

A week later we met Luscious Locks at the apartment to do the walkthrough and sign the lease. As he ambled from room to room filling out the form, I realized what made this seemingly cool guy not so douchey.

He was stupid.

I mean that in a nice way. Actually, I guess there's not a nice way to call someone stupid. But for real, this guy was a few beers short of a six pack.

While the walkthrough checklist was plastered with an incredible number of checkboxes and lines, it didn't need to get the better of him. Either start at the front of the house or the top of the form and work your way through, dude! Eventually you'll finish.

But no, he ping-ponged from room to room, first counting the number of outlets, then the number of light switches, then making one last round to count the doors. I can't imagine there's really a section on the form asking for this information. What are we going to do? Steal a light switch? And get away with it because it wasn't noted on the form?

"Ma'am, did you steal the light switch that used to be in this gaping hole?" the landlord would say upon check-out.

"Nope. And there's no way you can prove it either! Mwahahahaha! If only you had thought to count the light switches before we moved in. Joke's on you, sucker!"

Interestingly, the form didn't ask if the light switches and outlets actually worked. Which would have been infinitely more useful, considering (as we found out later) the apartment had its share of electrical issues.

For starters, one of the outlets in the living room didn't work. The only other outlet was connected to the light switch. That meant you had to plug everything into one power strip and turn it all on at once.

But even better were the bathroom light switches.

In Paris, it's common to have a *toilettte*, a room with a toilet that may or may not contain a sink. Then you'll have a separate *salle de bain* (bathroom) or *salle d'eau* (shower room) which will have a sink if the *toilettte* didn't, and may even have a sink if the *toilette* did. This means you have way more doors and sinks taking up space in your little apartment than necessary. And for some inexplicable reason, most French people prefer it this way.

Anyway, in our wonderful apartment, when you switched on the light in the *toilette* it turned out the light in the *salle de bain*. And vice versa. Maybe they assumed the tenants wouldn't ever use both at the same time?

Fortunately Mika's uncle Bruno fixed the problems soon after we moved in. But it didn't change the fact that Luscious Locks missed it on the walkthrough. Shame on me for not checking everything but I was too busy mentally making fun of the agent for counting outlets.

I guess I got what I deserved.

We made our way to the kitchen and Luscious Locks had the foresight to verify that the conduction stove worked. His preferred method for testing was to turn on the stove and then PLACE HIS HAND ON THE BURNER. My eyes popped out of their sockets as I watched in horror. Mika's eyes had already completely left his head.

"Um, I'm not sure that's the best way to test," Mika said.

Luscious Locks laughed. "I know! It's not even working. It turns off whenever I put my hand on it. There has to be a better way."

I stared in disbelief. So he agreed he shouldn't be testing it with his hand, but not for the right reason?

"What if you take one of those," Mika suggested, pointing to a stack of pots the previous tenant had left, "and set it on the stove? I think the stove doesn't work unless you have a pot on it. It's a safety feature."

Made sense to me.

But Luscious Locks didn't hear. He just kept repeating the same process. It reminded me of those public service announcements they used to air during commercial breaks from cartoons. "Don't try this at home!" they would warn, while we kids rolled our eyes, saying "As if," and then begged for the cartoons to come back on. Two-year-olds have mastered this concept.

After the fifth attempt, Luscious Locks gave up. "I'm sorry guys, it's broken."

"Mind if I try something?" Mika gently pushed past the guy and grabbed one of the pots. He set it on a burner, turned the stove on, then waited a few seconds. Then he turned it off, lifted the pot, and held his hand a few inches from the bottom of the pot. "It's warm. I think it works."

Luscious Locks looked as if Harry Potter had just cast the Incendio spell. "Wow, you're like *really* smart."

That makes one of you, dude.

Mika gave me a look that said "Can you believe this guy?"

I shot him a look back that said, "No, he's unreal."

We'd been married six brief months but had already established a way to make fun of people right in front of them without words. It's an incredibly useful skill when apartment-hunting in France.

"I think we're finished!" Luscious Locks was so proud of himself. Awww. "Anything else before we go?"

"If I could use the bathroom, that would be great." I figured I should check that the toilet flushed, plus, as a pregnant lady, I pretty much always had to go to the bathroom.

I passed five outlets and three light switches before reaching the *toilette* at the front of the house. I turned on the light (not noticing that it had turned off the light in the *salle de bain*) and started to close the door.

Wow, this bathroom was small.

I managed to close the door, undo my jeans, and sit on the toilet while only bumping the door and sink twenty-five times. My knees were one inch from the door.

Seriously, this bathroom was small.

But the toilet flushed. And we'd already signed the

lease. Home, sweet tiny home.

༺∾༻

A week later we were moved in and Bruno had fixed our electrical problems. Catherine swung by with croissants to have a peek.

"I got you this," she said, handing me a huge bag from a posh baby store. I unwrapped gift after gift until I was buried in onesies, blankets, and stuffed animals.

"Merci," I said, wondering where I'd find room for all this stuff. It was a good problem to have.

Mika gave her the tour, then they met me back in the kitchen where only a few crumbs indicated there had ever been any croissants.

"Sorry, I couldn't help myself," I said sheepishly, in the hopes it came across as an apology even though I wasn't really that sorry. You shouldn't leave me in a room with a bag of croissants if you don't want me to eat them all.

"No, no, chérie! I got them all for you! And that beautiful grandbaby. I'll bring more next time." I love my mother-in-law.

"So," she continued, "speaking of the baby, where is he or she going to sleep?"

She raised a good question. Our apartment was large overall (well, relatively speaking) but it only had one miniscule bedroom. Good thing I'd had years of experience organizing small spaces.

"We're going to keep the baby in a bassinet next to our bed at first. Did you happen to see the large armoire in the bedroom? We're going to use one side for us, one for the baby. There's room in there for a changing table, diapers, clothes, and blankets. It's nice that the previous tenants left it here. Now all the baby stuff will be in one place."

I had been rambling because Catherine was giving me a weird look and I didn't know how to handle it. Was it my

French? Had I made a mistake? Wouldn't be the first time I was totally off the mark.

"Hrm." She hesitated. "Are you sure that's a good idea?"

Did she know who she was talking to? I once lived in a 20 square meter apartment (215 square feet) that was so organized I was able to trick my friends into helping me move, without them realizing it would necessitate 30 trips up and down five flights of stairs. They thought I only had a few pairs of jeans and a plant.

"I think it's a great idea, if I do say so myself. We don't have much space here so I don't see a better way." I said it nicely but I couldn't help wonder what her concern was. Did she doubt my organizational skills? Obviously we'd like a two-bedroom apartment but that was out of our budget. This was our only option.

"Well, I… maybe it's not my place to say, but…"

"Mom, just spit it out," Mika said.

"I don't think the baby should sleep in the closet."

Mika and I paused for a second before bursting out laughing. "Mom! Who said anything about sleeping in the closet? We're going to keep the changing table and other baby stuff in there, but the baby will sleep in a bassinet next to our bed."

As I followed the conversation I noticed that while I understood what Mika had said, it wasn't phrased exactly the way I had said it. Somewhere along the lines I must have said something just enough off that it went over Catherine's head, while Mika, who was used to my French (and already knew the plan) had understood.

"Don't worry, Catherine," I said, still laughing, "I promise I won't put your grandbaby in the armoire."

She looked noticeably relieved. I couldn't believe she had actually thought I would make my baby sleep in the closet, but then I guess *she* couldn't believe I would actually make my baby sleep in the closet!

Amazing that after all this time in France, I could still make such a confusing mistake.

"OK, well, I better get going," she said, rising and giving us the family's customary four kisses on the cheek. "Sleeping in the armoire," she said, half under her breath. "You guys are never going to let me live this down."

And now I'm writing about it. She's going to kill me.

6

Maternity Leave

BY THE TIME I ANNOUNCED my pregnancy to my boss, I had been employed at my French company about a year. I hadn't quite gotten used to the lax French working style and the fact that they only actually work about half the year, once you factor in national holidays, a minimum of five weeks' vacation, and coffee breaks.

So I was shocked to learn I would be getting sixteen weeks of maternity leave. What would I do with all that time? Sure, take care of my baby. But as someone who has worked since age 14, the prospect of four months *sans travail* was hard to imagine.

The typical set-up is six weeks before the due date and ten weeks after. Unlike many American women who work up until their due date (because of an inflexible job or financial concerns or simply wanting to conserve their minimal maternity leave for after the baby arrives), the French really want expecting mothers to take it easy before the birth. And considering France has a lower rate of premature births than the U.S., they're probably right.

According to the official maternity book I received at my first prenatal appointment, French health officials have determined that six weeks before the due date is the ideal time to give mama some rest and reduce the risk of a preemie. Any longer is usually unnecessary and any shorter can be risky.

I, of course, didn't heed this advice.

My company's business was seasonal in nature and Christmas was our busiest period. Therefore, no one was allowed to take vacation around the holidays. But I couldn't stomach the thought of spending yet another Christmas apart from my American family.

I ran some numbers. I was due on September 17th, so if I could convince my boss to let me leave only three weeks early instead of six (which is the latest, by law, that you're allowed to work), then I'd have thirteen weeks after the baby was born, meaning I wouldn't come back to work until December 17th—smack dab in the middle of the holiday season. I would probably be allowed to take vacation because, honestly, if they hadn't sorted themselves out by the 17th, they were screwed anyway. Why make me return to work and miss my Christmas if it wouldn't help them?

"Does that sound OK?" I asked my boss, Laurent, and the general manager, Guillaume.

"Christmas is our busiest period. We need you. Take it as a compliment for how much we value you!" Laurent chuckled.

I didn't want a compliment, I wanted to visit my family, you fool.

Guillaume smoothly jumped in before I let a snarky comment slip out. "That sounds reasonable and will allow you time to finish your projects before you leave. But remember, this is an exception to the rule and I expect you to treat it as such."

You mean, next time I'm pregnant I can't go home for Christmas? Deal. We could cross that bridge when we came to it.

"Thank you, Guillaume. I really appreciate it."

Now I just had to keep that baby in until August 27th!

৵৶

The phone rang three times, then went to voice mail. "Hi Mom, it's Vicki," I began

"Hello?" Doug picked up mid-sentence. Standard practice in my parents' house. Allergic to calls from telemarketers, my mom and step-dad never answer the phone unless they recognize the caller ID. And my French number showed up differently each time for some reason, so they could never be sure it was really me and not someone trying to sell them snake oil. A few times I'd tried to jerk their chain by acting like a telemarketer, but given how often I called, the joke had gotten old pretty quickly. Now I knew to just start talking to the answering machine until they'd vetted my call.

"Hi Doug, how are you?"

"Good, good. Hold on, here's your mom."

"Honey? Hi! Everything OK with the baby?"

Parents always assume the worst.

"Yep, going well. Good news—my Christmas vacation got approved. I only get one week but it's better than nothing."

"Fantastic! The whole family can't wait to see you. Oh, and that reminds me, I booked my ticket to come visit. It's for the last week in September."

"Perfect. Everyone should be out of the hospital by then. So Doug isn't coming?"

"No, he's not up for the trip because of his circulation problems. The long plane ride is going to be a killer."

We chatted a while longer, though it always amazed me

we had anything to say when we emailed every day and commented on each other's Facebook statuses minutes after they were posted.

"I'd better call Dad. Once he knows you've booked your tickets he'll probably book his right away. You know how competitive Italians are."

I dialed the Florida number and he picked up on the first ring.

"Well hello! This must be my lovely daughter. To what do I owe this honor?"

He always greeted me that way even though I called every Sunday. But hey, if he thought it was an honor to talk to me I'd go ahead and let him think that.

"Just wanted to say hi. And let you know that Mom booked her ticket for the last week of September. You and Marsha can come any time after that."

Marsha was my sweet step-mom, who already had a bunch of grandbabies from her own four kids, but was still eager to meet her soon-to-be addition.

"OK, so should we book for the first week of October? Will the weather still be nice? And can we stay with you in your new apartment?"

Dad always asked questions in threes, making it a race to answer them all before he fired off more.

"The weather will be nice in the beginning of October and we would love it if you stayed with us."

"What airline do you recommend? Should we book today? Do you need us to bring anything?"

"From Orlando I think American might be your best bet but you should check around. Book soon, though. And can you bring some mac and cheese?"

He'd brought twenty boxes of my favorite pasta with artificial cheese flavoring when they'd come for our wedding but those were long gone.

"Sure, no problem. Anything else? You doing OK? How's Mika?"

I loved talking to him, but Mama needed a nap after all those questions!

Still, I was super excited that my parents were coming to visit. It would help bridge the gap before my regrettably short Christmas vacation.

ৡৢ

"*Oui, bonjour?*" I said, answering a call from an unknown number on my cell phone. I was at work and shouldn't have been taking a personal call, but as it happened so rarely I decided to chance it. It could have been Johnny Depp calling from his vacation home in the south of France, which is totally worth getting in trouble for.

"*Oui, hâllo.* This is probably someone from the hospital but I'm talking super fast so you can't be sure. Now that you're past the five-month mark in your pregnancy, we'd like you to participate in a study with some weird name that you can't understand over the phone. Are you interested? The research from this study can help pregnant women and babies."

"Sure, I would love to help with your mysterious study. What do I need to do?"

"You need to do something—a word you've never heard of—but don't worry, it's non-intrusive."

"OK, sounds like I shouldn't be agreeing to this but I'm going to naively trust you."

"Great! I will mail you more information but as a quick overview, the study will compare the differences in gestational diabetes between women who are of normal weight and women who are obese. We appreciate your time. *Bonne journée!*"

"*Bonne journée,*" I chirped back.

I was happy to assist in their study. As a pregnant woman, I felt I owed it to society to help out. While pregnancy feels long to the blimped-out woman going through it, it actually only offers a brief window for researchers to conduct studies.

The geeky scientist in me was thrilled to take part. If I understood correctly, I just needed to share the results of my gestational diabetes test (which I had to take anyway) and then they could analyze them against the results of other women, comparing mine to those of obese women.

Wait a minute… I wasn't in the *obese* category, was I? In the U.S. I would be considered normal and my weight gain was on par for my pregnancy, though admittedly it touched the upper limits of acceptability.[3]

But thinking back on all the foxy French ladies in the waiting room at my prenatal appointments, I had a sinking feeling I'd been placed in the overweight category.

Oh well, too late now. I'd already agreed to the study. I suppose all data points are useful, even if they are disheartening.

ও৶৶

At my six-month check-up, the doctor from the study stopped in for a quick chat and confirmed I was in the normal group. Yay me! That merited a reward. Perhaps a croissant?

Once the doctor left, the *sage-femme* proceeded with our appointment. Business as usual—fill out ridiculous amounts of paperwork in an ever-growing dossier (they should weigh *that* at each visit!) and endure a ridiculous lack

---

[3] Completely unfairly, pregnant women in France are expected to gain roughly 20-27 pounds (9-12 kilos), while in the U.S. the norm is 25-35 pounds (roughly 11-16 kilos). Worse, when I Googled this information, I started to type *prendre kilos pendant grossesse* (gain weight during pregnancy) and it "completed" my search phrase by changing it to *perdre kilos pendant grossesse* (lose weight during pregnancy). They don't even want you indulging in research about weight gain!

of privacy in a room with no changing curtain, no paper sheet. Just me, the *sage-femme*, and the breeze blowing on my bare backside.

The one disconcerting piece of information was that my baby's head was already down in birthing position.

"It's not alarming for his head to be down this early but we need to keep an eye on it. And you need to limit your physical activity. Can you run me through a typical day for you?"

Piece of cake. I'd read in my pregnancy books that you shouldn't start any new exercise routine during pregnancy and that you should always stop if it hurts or you get too tired. I knew I wasn't overdoing it.

"Sure! In the morning I do some calisthenics while getting ready, like squats and leg lifts while brushing my teeth and doing my make-up."

Her eyes widened but she let me continue.

"Then it's a 10-minute walk to the Métro, a 35-minute ride where I sometimes find a seat, then a 15-minute walk from the Métro to my office. Oh, and I usually take the stairs when exiting the stations because the escalator is always backed up."

She looked about two seconds away from a heart attack but she kept scribbling in my dossier.

"After work, I meet my husband near his office and we walk home, which takes about an hour. So, as you can see, it's only a bit of walking and some calisthenics."

She set her pen down. "OK, here's how it's gonna be from now on. No calisthenics. You can walk to and from the Métro, but you need to find a seat while riding. As a pregnant woman you have the right to a seat so you just have to ask. And no more stairs, understood? You need to severely limit your exercise or the baby will come early and we don't want that."

I nodded, grimly envisioning all the pounds I would pack on with my reduced exercise regimen.

"If you don't listen to me, I will have to stop you from work early," she gently reprimanded.

"No! I can't stop work early! I need to continue as late as possible so I can spend Christmas with my family."

"Then keep that in mind the next time you're too shy to ask for a seat on the Métro or want to take a flight of stairs."

ॐॐ

"How did your appointment go?" Mika asked that night on our walk home from work.

"Fine. I'm in the normal group for the study."

"Ha, I'm sure you're relieved."

"Yeah. But the *sage-femme* said the baby's head is down low and I need to take it easy. I'm sure she's overreacting. You know how the French are, no offense."

"None taken, but maybe you should listen to her?"

"I did! I sat on the Métro and took the escalator instead of the stairs. She said walking is OK." Probably not for an hour but c'mon! I was a naturally active person and was having a hard enough time cutting out the activities she'd said to.

"OK, as long as you're sure," he said, draping an arm around my shoulders.

"I'm sure."

7

Hypochondria, Not Just for Frenchies

SEMI-FOLLOWING DOCTOR'S ORDERS, I reduced my exercise program and tried to slow down. But it wasn't easy.

While I did enjoy Mika rubbing my feet as I sprawled out on the couch, I wasn't quite comfortable asking him to refill my water glass or hand me my laptop or whatever other whim crossed my mind. It seemed so lazy.

And the American in me couldn't help but think it was a typical French overreaction on the part of the *sage-femme*.

The French are obsessed with obsessing over their health. There are more pharmacies than grocery stores; there's one on nearly every street. Few drugs are available over-the-counter, but after a brief consultation with the pharmacist, they will usually prescribe something (short of antibiotics or morphine) without requiring a trip to the doctor. It's admittedly convenient but almost too convenient for this nation of hypochondriacs.

So I'd taken the *sage-femme's* advice with a grain of salt.

Because while they say they don't want you to exercise, they still give you the evil eye at every kilo you gain. And considering the only thing France has more of than pharmacies is *boulangeries* filled with buttery, calorie-laden awesomeness, it's really unfair. How can I survive a waiting room full of skinny French pregnant ladies if I'm not allowed to exercise off my croissants?

"You're beautiful, honey," Mika said about a hundred times per day.

"Promise?"

"Promise."

"What if I do this?" I would test him by jiggling my booty and trying to strike a sexy pose, knowing full well how ridiculous it looked.

"Even better."

"OK, now I know you're lying."

"I'm not. I promise. You're a beautiful pregnant woman and you look healthy and perfect. Please stop worrying about it."

"Well… I'm pretty sure a foot rub would help me forget all about it."

"Deal."

This guy was too good to be true.

ഇൗ

"Are you sure of the date of your pregnancy?"

Mika and I were at our third ultrasound appointment and the doctor couldn't believe her eyes.

"Yes, I'm sure," I replied.

"And you've been tested for gestational diabetes?"

"Yes, and I don't have it."

"Well, you better get ready. This is going to be one big boy!"

At the previous ultrasound we'd found out we were having a boy. Yay! Actually, I would have been equally happy with a girl. I just wanted to know either way so that I could stop calling my baby "it" and start buying some stylish Parisian clothes for him.

The doctor glided the wand around my ever-growing belly, noting the essential measurements on the screen, letting out "Oh la la's" at the particularly large measurements.

"And I see his head is already in position. It's really low down, actually. Combined with his size, I wouldn't be surprised if this baby came early."

Again with the worrywarts! These people needed to chill. I'd read my pregnancy books and mostly followed the *sage-femme's* orders. I was practically an expert.

I wouldn't have minded if the baby came a tad early—I have a thing with birthdays and like the numbers to either be all odd or all even, and since it was 2012 I was shooting for even. So August would have been preferable to September for that all-important reason. But I wasn't going to wish for an early birth just for that.

No, better that he stay inside and cook as long as possible, even if it meant Mommy's chubby thighs were chafing from rubbing together in the relentless July heat.

೧৵৶

Not being allowed to drink, and not being able to stand the high temperatures, I'd taken a hiatus from the bars of Paris, particularly since few were air-conditioned. This meant I was severely lacking in the Anne Marie department. I needed a pick-me-up.

"Hello?"

"Hi Ammo, it's Vicki."

"Well hello there! How goes it with my pregnant friend? Is your ass getting huge?"

"You know it! So, have I missed anything good at the pub?"

"Nah, not really. I mean, there are always some good laughs but it's pretty much the same ol' same ol'."

That was good to hear. "Get this. We had the ultrasound the other day and the baby is huge. He's in the 90th percentile for nearly every measurement."

"Nearly? What part of him is small?"

I should have known she'd ask. "His femur is in the 34th percentile. Which is odd since the rest of his measurements are large, plus Mika is so tall."

"His femur or femurs, plural?"

"I just have the measurement for one."

"So maybe one of them is normal. Nothing to worry about!"

"Ammo! That's way worse! If his femur is short I'd want *both* of them to be short!" Man, I hadn't even thought about his femurs being different sizes from each other.

"Calm down, I'm only taking the piss. I'm sure he's fine."

I'd learned long ago from my Irish friend that "taking the piss" sounds bad but it just means "giving you a hard time." I traveled all this way to Paris to learn French and it turns out I still had some English phrases to learn.

"I'm sure you're right," I said, not entirely convinced. I pictured my poor baby walking around with one shoe bigger than the other to balance things out. I'm sure there were worse things in life but at that moment, it felt like the worst ever.

French hypochondria was rubbing off on me.

8

Rush Hour

"HOW'S THE FACEBOOK APP PROJECT GOING, Vicki?"
Guillaume asked one sweltering August afternoon.

Could it be any hotter in the office? I know I had an
excess of hormones coursing through my veins, not to
mention a nice-sized bump containing a healthy chunk of a
baby in it, but I couldn't be the only one who was
overheating.

That summer was one of the hottest in Paris history,
which was worse than it sounds. In St. Louis, people
complain about the heat, then hop in their air-conditioned
cars to drive to air-conditioned stores before returning to
their air-conditioned houses. My mom sometimes wears a
sweater to the grocery store in the dead of summer.

In Paris, you hop on the non-air-conditioned Métro,
enjoy everyone's unshowered body odor, then shop in non-
air-conditioned stores, then return to your non-air-
conditioned house.

Or non-air-conditioned office.

The three fans blowing in the open space did nothing to diminish the growing sweat stains in my armpits. And I was pretty sure my legs were stuck together.

"It's going well. Geoffrey finishes his internship at the end of the week and he should have the project wrapped up by then."

"Great work. How about we do a quick status meeting tomorrow morning, the three of us?"

Before I could answer he strode away in his fancy suit. Just looking at it made me sweat. I swept my hair in a ponytail and surveyed the situation.

Not much work remained on the project but now I needed to gather some notes for our meeting the next day. How could I be expected to work in this heat? Seriously, it was like 95 degrees outside and 94 degrees inside. The chocolates in my candy dish had melted into one big blob. Might as well eat the blob before diving in to work.

I could always catch up tomorrow.

ৎৣৄ

Rolling over on the sofa I glanced at the clock. Yikes, already 9:30. That was our new bedtime, because Mika and I were awesome.

Back in my partying days I usually hadn't even left the house at that point, preferring to down a few inexpensive glasses of wine at home before blowing my paycheck at the bars.

But now it was easier to go to bed at 9:30 than trying to stay up later to "be cool." I woke up at least three times a night to use the bathroom and had difficulty falling back asleep, so it was nice to have those extra hours of shut-eye built up.

Plus, as every parent, website, and book told me, "Sleep now because once the baby comes you won't sleep for years!" Oh, people are so clever.

"Hey Grandpa, let's brush our teeth and head to bed," I said to Mika.

He snapped awake, having dozed off in front of the soccer game. "I'm right behind you."

Once in bed we snuggled, my bump resting in the small of his back, our little baby boy kicking the both of us. Despite the heat we still liked to cuddle. Hey, I was just giving my French husband the affection he deserved, otherwise they'd take away my marriage certificate.

Pop! The heck?

My belly felt funny. I sat up to check the time—6:30 am. Boo. The alarm wouldn't go off until 7:00 but I knew I wouldn't get back to sleep now.

I couldn't tell exactly what was wrong. Probably just gas. Lying on my tummy would have felt so good but I had a big baby in my way. So I got on all fours, then laid my head on my pillow and tried to get comfortable. Oh the joys of pregnancy.

"It's a beautiful daaaaaaaay!" Bono blared from our radio. Man, that half hour had passed quickly.

"You know, it's smart of the DJs to pick songs like that to play in the morning when they know everyone will be grumpy and just waking up," I said to a half-asleep Mika.

"Grmpf."

I heard our automatic coffee maker go off in the kitchen. "Hey, why don't you stay here, honey? I'll grab you when the coffee's done."

I hopped out of bed as fast as my bump would allow and headed to the *toilette*. Then I waddled into the bathroom (so convenient to have to go to a different room, sigh) and started getting ready.

As I was washing my face, I felt something wet on my leg. Hrm, I must have been overzealous with the splashing.

I proceeded to brush my teeth and felt another slosh. Hold on, I couldn't be *that* sloppy.

Oh no. It had happened. The pregnancy books had prepared me for this day but I still didn't think it would come.

I had peed myself.

At least Mika hadn't seen and I was about to hop in the shower. But still, I was now Someone Who Had Peed Herself.

࿇

Actually, I must confess. I was already Someone Who Had Peed Herself. And not when I was a baby. Well, probably, but that doesn't count.

And not during a drunken night out, either. I'm a puker, not a pants-wetter.

No, this lovely episode happened in third grade during a statewide standardized four-hour test.

"Once the test booklets have been passed out, you may not leave the room for any reason until either everyone has finished or the time is up," Mrs. Schaeffer had instructed. I attended a Catholic grade school and while our teachers weren't nuns, Mrs. Schaeffer might as well have been one.

"Any questions? No? You may begin."

Considering I'd been teaching myself algebra from an 8th grade textbook I'd bought with my lunch money (guess how many friends I had), this exam was child's play. I loved school and I loved tests even more. I blew through it, finishing in slightly over an hour.

Luckily we were allowed to read while being held hostage, so I whipped out my latest Nancy Drew and dove in. Ah, three hours of uninterrupted sleuthing.

Except eventually I felt the need to go to the restroom. I held it as long as I could but when I glanced at the clock and saw that more than an hour remained, I knew I wouldn't make it.

Slowly, I approached Mrs. Schaeffer's desk, trying to minimize my motions so as not to disturb my bursting-at-the-seams bladder.

"May I please be excused to go to the restroom?"

"You heard the rules, Vicki. No exceptions. Go back to your seat." She resumed reading her book, probably a manual titled "50 Different Ways to Cook Children Who Misbehave."

"But I really have to go! I already handed in my test. Please?"

She didn't even look up from her book. I returned to my seat and considered my options. There was no way I could hold it for another hour. And there was no way Mrs. S was going to break the rules.

I only had one option.

Without going into detail[4], let me just say I was thankful for the dark maroon hue and busy plaid of our uniforms. Sure, anyone with half a sense of smell would be able to detect what had happened, but at least I could hide it from the casual observer.

I passed the rest of the hour trying to join Nancy Drew in her adventures, but instead dreamt up ways to embarrass Mrs. Schaeffer every time I got a whiff of pee.

While I was no stranger to peeing my pants, it didn't mean I liked it. If this pregnant lady was already losing control, what would it be like after I'd endured labor and

---

[4] You can thank my editors for that. The very same editors who encouraged me to tone down the airplane vomit story in my first book. I couldn't bear to part with such masterpieces, so I have two Word files tucked away on my computer, one titled "Vomit" and one titled "Pee." If a hacker ever got ahold of my computer he'd probably back up real slowly and shake his head in disgust.

delivery? I envisioned coughing during a client meeting and peeing my pants. Laughing at one of Anne Marie's stories and peeing my pants.

I shuddered.

Best not to think of my future. Just focus on the present. I needed to jump in the shower and get ready for work. Maybe even leave early so I could prepare for the meeting with Guillaume.

I was in and out of the shower in record time. "Honey, the coffee's done. I'll be in the kitchen."

Mika started to get out of bed, so I felt comfortable leaving him. I poured a cup of coffee and booted up my computer. I had just logged on to Facebook when I felt another trickle.

You have got to be kidding me!

It had been bad enough when it happened before my shower but this was plain gross. The Incredible Peeing Lady couldn't even drink a cup of coffee without making a mess.

I walked to the *salle de bain*, peeked in and saw that Mika was in the shower, then went to the *toilette* before returning to my computer.

Pulling up Google, I typed "Did I pee my pants or did my water break" and hit enter.

I was 99% sure I had just peed myself—I was still six weeks shy of my due date[5]. Even though the *sage-femme* and ultrasound doctor had said my baby might come early, I

---

[5] The French due date is one week later than the American due date because it's calculated for a 41-week pregnancy instead of 40. I thought this was ridiculous at first (you can't just add a week, you crazies!) until I learned there's actually a good reason. Since the health care system pays for your maternity leave, they need to have some sort of standard across pregnancies, which are of course unique and unpredictable. By using 41 weeks they know that for sure you'll have the baby by that date, because if you don't, the *sage-femme* will induce labor. So I could say I was only 5 weeks away from my due date but that's not as dramatic, is it?

didn't believe it.

Google returned over 10,000 results. At least I wasn't alone.

I clicked on the first one, where a panicked mom-to-be posed her question to the forum:

```
I'm 37 weeks pregnant and I think I
peed my pants. But maybe the baby is
coming early and it was actually my water
breaking? How do I know? Help!
```

The page of responses all had the same gist:

```
Girl, get yourself to the hospital!
Your water broke.
```

OK, but she was 37 weeks pregnant. I was only 35 weeks. Totally different. I clicked on another search result:

```
How do you know if your water broke or
if you peed yourself?
```

My question exactly! The forum's responses were again similar in nature:

```
Girlfriend, if you have to ask, then
your water broke. Go to the hospital.
```

OK, but maybe these women had never peed themselves before. I had and I knew. Actually... when I peed in Mrs. Schaeffer's classroom, it was a lot wetter than this. And it smelled like pee, not water.

One more click, though, just to be sure:

```
I think my water broke but just in case
I only peed myself, I don't want to go to
the hospital and have them send me home,
laughing that I peed myself.
```

The forum's answer? You guessed it:

```
Girl, what are you doing writing on
forums when you should be GOING TO THE
HOSPITAL? They won't laugh. Just GO.
```

Damn. Where was the forum saying "Girl, finish your coffee and go to work and have your meeting like planned?" Because that was all I wanted to hear.

"Hey, whatcha reading?" Mika asked, as he entered the kitchen and poured himself a cup of coffee. "You look engrossed."

"How does a Frenchman know words like 'engrossed'? I will never know how to say that in French. Unless it's on-gross-ay?" Hey, it worked sometimes—just say an English word with a French accent.

"Oh my god, no. It does not mean the same thing at all. You probably shouldn't repeat that word."

"Why? What does it mean?"

"I'm not going to tell you but it's really vulgar."

Yikes. I thought back to how many times over the years I'd tried that technique on various words. Oh boy. I'd probably unknowingly offended half the nation by now.

"What were we talking about anyway?" he said.

I remembered where our conversation had been going, but I didn't want to bring him back on track. He would make me go to the hospital and I already had 10,000 women on the internet shouting at me to do the same. Couldn't I finish my coffee in peace? And besides, what were the chances I was actually going into labor?

"Um, Vicki? You still there?"

"Yes, sorry." Seeing his concerned face, I knew I had to tell him. This was his baby, too. "So, no big deal, but either I peed myself or my water broke."

His eyes widened to cartoon proportions.

"The internet is telling me to go to the hospital…"

Before I could finish he got up and paced the room.

"Let's go! Right now!" He picked up his satchel then set it down again. He looked around the room, lost.

"OK," I agreed. "I'm sure it's nothing but I guess we should check it out. Hopefully I can still make it to work on time. I have to prepare for that stupid meeting with Guillaume."

He chugged the rest of his coffee, burning his mouth. "I can't believe you can think about work at a time like this."

"I'm just being realistic. They will probably tell me I peed myself and will release me, and then I'm gonna have a huge day of work ahead of me. Better to be prepared."

Ha, "prepared." That would turn out to be quite the joke.

Confessions Before Baby #1

During the summer between my sophomore and junior year of college, I scored an actuarial internship in Seattle. True, my aunt and uncle both worked at the behemoth insurance company and put in a good word for me, but my high GPA and letters of recommendation sealed the deal.

Since I had to relocate clear to the other side of the country, bringing my kitten, Zero, was not an option. Thankfully, my boyfriend's sisters agreed to care for her during my absence.

Fast forward to the end of the summer when my boyfriend and I were ready to head back to the University of Missouri to start our third year of higher education.

"All set, Mark?" I asked him, hopping in my teal blue sedan that had just been repaired with all my hard-earned internship money.

"Yep, good to go!"

We embarked on the 100-mile drive to Columbia, windows rolled down, singing along to a mixed CD I'd made for the occasion. Cruising along the highway, we spotted more farmhouses, fields, and rolling hills with each passing mile.

"I can't wait to get settled," I said. "I have so much unpacking to do."

"Same here. It's amazing how much junk I brought home for the summer," Mark said, glancing at the overflowing backseat.

"I know. I hope I didn't forget anything."

As if. I was the world's most organized person! No way would I forget anything.

I planned to unpack the minute I arrived and organize everything the first day. Then I could unwind on the futon, curl up next to my…

Oh. My. God. "I forgot Zero!"

"I was wondering when you were going to realize that."

"What! You *knew*?"

"You *didn't*?"

He had a point, but still. "How could you let me leave her behind?"

"How could you just *leave her behind*? I realized you had forgotten her but figured if she was really important to you, you would have remembered. She's better off with my sisters anyway. You know you're not supposed to have pets in your apartment, plus Zero's already gotten used to living with the girls."

I couldn't believe he'd essentially made the decision for me. But worse, I couldn't believe I left my cat behind. Who does that?

If I was capable of forgetting a sweet little kitten, what about my sweet little baby? Would we go on a walk, only for me to get distracted and leave him alone in his stroller? Would I step out to run an errand and forget my child sleeping in his bed? What kind of mother was I going to be if I couldn't keep track of my own cat?

"I don't really have a good defense. I suck. I guess I just spent so much time away from her and then was so busy ever since I got back from Seattle that it never crossed my mind. You're right, she's probably better off with your sisters than me."

Still, that was a tough pill to swallow.

9

Dazed and Confused

BY THE SEVEN-MONTH MARK, I'd scoured my French and English pregnancy books. My inbox pinged daily with mommy-to-be newsletters and I received loads of unsolicited, well-meaning advice from friends and strangers. The common theme among these recommendations was that I should prepare my hospital bag now.

I hear you, guys, but is your apartment the size of a thimble? I was already bumping into the kitchen countertops every time I turned around and could barely edge along the bed for my thrice-nightly bathroom breaks. If I packed a suitcase I'd surely trip over it every five minutes.

Plus, isn't seven months a little extreme? Two months early, people? Really?

Yes, really.

When Mika and I rushed to the hospital that morning, I had no idea they were going to keep me there until the baby came. I hadn't really thought my water had broken (it had) and I was sure I could go to work as usual (I couldn't).

I hadn't even eaten breakfast. My stomach growled. I was one grouchy bitch.

A bitch without a suitcase.

"Hello again," the smiling *sage-femme* said as she entered the monitoring room in the ER. "Let's see how you're progressing."

The fetal monitor beeped rhythmically while the Richter scale (at least that's what it looked like) printed out my contractions. Since my water had indeed broken, I had to be hospitalized until the baby came in order to minimize risk of infection. It was possible the baby could stay in until the 37-week mark, at which point he would be considered full-term.

But given the rate of my contractions, which were repeating like quakes along a fault line, that seemed pretty unlikely.

I whipped out my phone. "Hi, Guillaume? It's Vicki. I just wanted to let you know that I'll be missing our meeting today. I'll call Geoffrey in a minute to brief him." I sighed. "I'm in the hospital until this baby comes. It could be today or it could be in two weeks."

"No worries about the meeting. As for the baby, I'll hold out hope that he comes in two weeks, but in my experience—and remember, I have four kids—this baby is probably coming today. Just a little friendly advice so you can mentally prepare."

There was that word again—prepare! I was usually the world's most prepared person. For my wedding, I'd created a Wedding Welcome Packet full of tips and maps and optional planned activities for my out-of-town guests during the week leading up to the wedding. I always had at least twenty boxes of mac and cheese stocked in my pantry. I was never more than a day behind on my pedicure and rarely left the house unless the floor was clean enough to eat off of (though, if you ate off my floors I'd smack you for messing them up).

Prepared was my middle name!

Which made it hard to deal with the fact that my baby might be coming early. And that I hadn't even eaten yet. And that I didn't have a bag packed with my essentials. The only solution was to not have the baby today.

"Looks like you're having this baby today!" The *sage-femme* placed a delicate hand on my arm. "Don't worry. You're in one of France's best hospitals for neonatal care. Everything will be fine. Now, let's get you over to the exam room so they can see how much you're dilating."

ঌণ্ড

After being transferred to the sterile examination room where they confirmed the labor was most definitely in progress, they transferred me to a comfy hospital room where I could wait it out.

"I'm starving," I said to Mika, holding his hand as we cuddled on the hospital bed.

"Me too. But I don't want to leave you."

"Yeah, I want you to stay here. We can worry about it later."

Contractions were still so painless and far apart that I hardly noticed them. We had some time to kill, but I was convinced it would end up going quickly. I took after my mom in many ways and both of her deliveries were under four hours.

"Who knows, we could be outta here in a couple hours!" I said. "My water broke at 6:30 this morning and it's noon now, so it could happen quickly. I'm gonna call my parents."

I started with my dad, since he was on the East Coast.

"Hi honey! To what do I owe this honor?" he answered, clearly having already downed one cup of coffee.

Mom certainly wouldn't have been that chipper at 6:00 am.

I filled him in on the situation. "So, it looks like we'll be having our little guy today," I said.

"Have contractions started yet?"

"Funny you mention it, but I just had my first big one."

"While we were talking?"

"Yeah. Clearly contractions are not as bad as everyone makes them out to be if I can talk through them." Oh, how the gods would smite me down later for saying that! "Well, I'd better call Mom. Hopefully I don't give her a heart attack calling this early. Love you."

"Love you, too! Keep us posted!"

I glanced over at Mika, whose eyes were like saucers.

"Did you say you had a contraction? Like a real one?"

"Yeah, but that's what's supposed to happen. No biggie. It wasn't even that painful. We're right on track. You can relax."

"Ha, relax. Sure." He stood up and paced the room. "I still don't know what to do about food or going home to get the suitcase. It seems like things could happen any minute, you know?"

"I know. This is so awkward. Why didn't I pack the damn bag? The ONE time in my life I'm not prepared."

"I'm never going to let you live this down."

"Yeah, don't. That was really stupid of me."

౿◦ぬ

I dialed my mom's number and prepared to leave a message.

"Hello? Is everything alright?" My mom was unable to hide the panic from her voice.

"Wow, I think that's the first time you ever answered without letting it go to voicemail!"

"Well it's 5:30 in the morning. I was worried. Are you OK?"

I'd been holding it together all morning but now that I had my mom on the phone, my voice cracked with emotion. "Um, well, I'm kind of having my baby today."

"Aren't you only 35 weeks along? Is it serious? What happened?"

She'd stolen my dad's trademarked three-question-rapid-fire. "Yeah, it's early but they think it will be OK. Contractions have started so this whole thing might be over with very soon. Oh, the *sage-femme* just walked in, I have to go. I'll keep you updated!" I quickly hung up the phone and turned to the *sage-femme*.

"Bonjour, Madame Lesage. You are now feeling contractions?"

"Yes. They're not that painful and they're still about five minutes apart."

"OK, we're going to transfer you to the labor room and you'll stay there until it's time to deliver. We are also waiting for the results of your blood test this morning to see if we can administer the epidural. I assume you still want one?"

In France, epidurals are standard procedure. The attitude is "why suffer if you don't have to." In the U.S. there's this whole movement (at least, from what I could tell by the pregnancy forums I couldn't tear myself away from) where women think it's better to not have one and almost wear it like a badge.

Considering my contractions were mild, and hoping that my labor would be speedy like both of my mom's, I didn't think I'd need an epidural.

"I'd like to have the option but I don't think I'll need one."

She and Mika both gave me a look that said, "Just like you thought you didn't need the suitcase." But at least they were nice enough to not say it out loud.

∽✌

Once in the sparse labor room, time passed weirdly. The mid-afternoon sun peeked through the tiny windows, but it did little to brighten the gray walls.

My contractions came stronger and faster, but it seemed like only a few minutes had passed. You'd think time would pass slowly if you were enduring something so unpleasant, but I guess I just didn't know what to think. It sort of hurt, but wasn't as bad as I expected.

I felt happy (I was going to have a baby!) but also disappointed that I hadn't been able to keep him in longer. And I was worried about his health.

Before I knew it, three hours had passed and the pain had now reached medieval torture levels. Mika seemed to be in an equal amount of pain just having to watch. He was literally on the edge of his seat.

"Is there anything I can do to help?"

"Not unless you want to *bleep-bleep-the-bleepin'-bleep*." I don't remember what I actually said but I know it wasn't suitable for all audiences.

He slid his phone out of his pocket right as a contraction from hell hit.

"Put the *bleeping* phone away!" I screamed.

He rammed the phone back in his pocket. "I'm sorry. I was just going to queue up the Vicki Delivery Playlist. I thought that would help."

The contraction subsided. "Um… so… yeah. Sorry about that. Music is a great idea. I'm sorry I yelled."

"Is everything OK in here?" The *sage-femme* shared Mika's worried expression. "I heard yelling."

"I'm sorry. The pain is becoming unbearable. Any chance I can get that epidural anytime soon?"

She held back a smile but I saw the corners of her mouth curve slightly upward. "I'll go check on your results. We'll administer it as soon as possible. But remember, it can take up to an hour from the time the decision is made to the time it takes effect. You'll have to find a way to manage the pain until then." Meaning, "Don't yell at your husband or you'll make it worse."

Mercifully, the blood results came back and I was good to go. By the time they shot that glorious needle into my back, it'd been twelve hours since my water broke and many hours of pain. Now I definitely wasn't getting any food, and Mika didn't want to leave the hospital to pack my bag.

We were trapped until this baby came.

Hours passed and still no baby. At least the pain had been masked but, um, I thought my baby had been in a hurry to come early? What the heck was he doing? Smoking a cigarette and reading the newspaper? Let's get this show on the road!

Mika and I drifted in and out of sleep as best as we could in the hospital room. As doctors and nurses and *sage-femmes* came in to check on me, I noticed their faces had changed. Huh? Oh yeah, it must be the night shift staff.

So much for a quick labor.

❦

At about 9:00 pm, my new *sage-femme* came in for the finger check. Oh goodie.

"Nice! We're ready to go!" she announced.

I beamed a smile at Mika. Though I'd been half-asleep moments earlier, I perked up at her compliment. Who's good at dilating? I am! I deserved a gold star. Or at least a cookie. I'd settle for a baby.

They transferred me to the delivery room. Show time!

Or not.

Hours ticked by while Mika dozed on and off in his cozy armchair and I slept the best I could in the dim light, considering I was hooked up to all sorts of machines and people came in every ten minutes to check on me.

"You know, now that we've made it this far, I'd almost

rather the baby comes after midnight. That way his birthday is even."

I was afraid Mika would think that was the dumbest thing he'd ever heard, but no, my husband confirmed why I married him. "That would be awesome! And then his birthday would be my half-birthday! And the anniversary of when we met!"

"And then I would never mix up the date in French!"

You see, France (and pretty much the entire rest of the world besides the U.S.) writes the date as day-month-year. It seems to make sense—you start with the smallest unit of time and increase.

But I'm with the U.S. on this one, and not just because I'm American. When gauging the timing of something, knowing the month first is more useful, then the date. Two events occurring in the same month are much more relevant than two events occurring on the same date. What on earth can I do with the information "It's on the 23rd?" But at least if I know it's in March, I have an idea if I'm free or not before you even tell me the day.

Furthermore, when I'm organizing files, I'm rarely going to want to see all the documents created on the 23rd of every month, but I could be interested in viewing everything created in March. When sorting a directory, it's infinitely more helpful to have the month first, then the day.

In fact, the way most computer programmers code the date is YYYY-MM-DD. Since the year is such a large unit of time, we generally know what year it is and don't need to specify it. So the next most useful measurement is the month.

Just to make sure the horse is really and truly beaten, how do you browse a calendar? Month first, right? Take *that*, rest of the world. It *does* make sense for the month to come before the day[6].

I do realize we're talking about a microsecond before you then learn either the day or the month, but I still maintain that the American way is better.

Anyhoo, this is one of those things that I just can't get right, despite being an analytical math nerd (see above paragraphs for proof of nerdiness and overthinking). My birthday may be 24/10/1980 in France but that will never look right to me.

And so if my son's birthday were to be August 7th, I would likely write 8/7/2012 on government forms and French officials would think I meant July 8th and he would get held back from school or imprisoned for fraud, all because his American mom is a dummy. If he could hold on another 10 minutes or so, his birthday would be 8/8 in any country and it would be one less thing for Mama to worry about.

No worries, he held on.

I figured I'd squeeze in a quick phone call to Mom before I lost my chance.

"Hi honey, you have that baby yet?" she asked.

"Nope, but I think it's gonna happen in the next half hour. I wanted to call before things got crazy because I don't know when I'll have another chance."

"Thanks, sweetie. You know I appreciate the updates. I've been running around work all day telling anyone who will listen that my daughter is having her baby today. August 7th. That's a nice birthday."

"Actually, Mom, it's already August 8th here. So that

---

[6] A footnote? After all this? I just have one final point to make. I believe the basis for the difference is due to linguistics. In the U.S. we say "March 23rd," which is the active voice, much like how we tend to express everything. The French, and many other populations, verbalize the date more passively as "the 23rd of March." So each country's way of writing the date simply reflects the way they speak it. Making it easier to understand why they do it, even if I still think the month should come before the day. OK, I promise I'm done with this subject.

will be his birthday."

"Oh how funny! He's going to be born in a few minutes but it's still only August 7th here. I'll be telling people his birthday is August 8th when it's not even August 8th yet!" She was getting a real kick out of this. I felt sorry for her co-workers who were going to have to hear *that* story the rest of the day.

"OK, well, I better get going. Can you pass the word on to Dad? I'll call you both as soon as I can. Love you!"

At 12:15 am, the *sage-femme* returned and said it was go time. A nurse, a student (how many students did they have in this damn hospital?), and a pediatrician followed her in, and the world stared at my business while I pushed. I would have been embarrassed but at this stage in the game I was just happy it was almost over.

After a few pushes, the *sage-femme* scooped up my baby boy and plopped him on my bouncy belly before doing whatever it is they do after the birth (I'll spare you the details since I don't even want to think about them myself).

I was so weak from being in labor for 18 hours and being all epiduraled-up that I was afraid to move him. So I just held my baby in a funny-shaped ball on my belly, Mika's arms wrapped around us, until they came to take my little guy away. As a preemie, he'd need to have extra tests and would likely have to be on machines all night long.

Those twenty seconds with my baby were all I got for the next few hours but they were the best twenty seconds of my life.

10

The Boss

THIRTY QUARTER POUNDERS. 3,750 M&M's. $150 in quarters. What do these have in common (besides the fact that I want them all right now)?

They weigh 7.5 pounds, same as my six-week premature baby.

Preemies come in many sizes, but they're usually not that big. In fact, only 40% of all babies born weigh 7.5 pounds or more. So when we went to see Leonardo Quentin Lesage for the first time in the NICU, Mika and I were shocked.

Surrounded by miniature babies hooked up to respirators and feeding tubes, my ginormous baby looked out of place. Though he was still hooked up to a respirator and feeding tube. Since he was born early, his lungs needed a little help getting enough oxygen. And since he was born huge, the poor guy wore himself out every time he ate, making it hard to get enough food to sustain his big body. The feeding tube ensured he got his fill in case he fell asleep during a meal.

"We call him The Boss," the nurse said, as she proceeded to explain the machines to us and demonstrate how we could safely hold our son with all those wires attached to him.

"You come into my house on the day my daughter is to be married and you ask me to murder," I said to Mika in my best Marlon Brando.

"I'm gonna make him an offer he can't refuse," Mika countered.

"I am the boss, the Godfather," I said before catching the nurse's eye.

"If you're done, you can hold him now," the nurse said. "And if he wakes up you can try to nurse him." She was nice about it but I could tell she thought we weren't taking the situation seriously.

If I took it seriously, I would probably burst into tears. True, my baby boy was big and relatively healthy, but he was hooked up to an alarming number of machines, and I had trouble following her explanations (in French, of course) after 18 hours of labor the previous day and four hours of restless sleep. A few quotes from the Godfather were the only thing keeping me from a full-on breakdown.

Holding my sweet little baby was an amazing feeling. I ran my fingers through his full head of dark hair (still a bit greasy from the delivery, adding to his tough-guy Mafia look) and over his olive skin. Against my pale skin and blond hair, this baby totally didn't look like mine. He looked exactly like his handsome daddy.

❧

We quickly got used to life in the NICU. What choice did we have? Leo would be in there for at least a week or two, so we made ourselves comfortable.

The knowledgeable staff was super helpful, teaching us

how to bathe him, feed him, and change him. I had years of experience in babysitting but it was different with my own baby. I guess the tubes and wires played a part. But it was also just so sudden. I wasn't prepared.

The weekend rolled around and that's when I learned that the best people worked the coveted weekday shifts and the craptastic employees were stuck with the Saturday night shift.

As the sun set and the last of the familiar faces left, two weirdoes from the night crew entered our room and introduced themselves.

"Hi, I'm Jeanine the Smoking Machine. I smoked a pack of cigarettes before my shift and in fact one might still be burning in my pocket. I'm nice but my aroma really stands out against this sterile environment." Her husky voice was surprisingly pleasing, but she had a smoky fog surrounding her, like a cigarette-toting version of Pig Pen.

"And I'm Serge, proud owner of the world's worst toupee. I'm not even sure I have a medical degree. I'm not wearing a badge. In fact, I might be lost but who cares? This seems like a fun place to spend a Saturday night."

Mika had been holding Leo and I'd been mid-sentence. We were both left with our jaws hanging wide open at these two characters.

I guess they would have to do. Surely the hospital wouldn't allow them in the Neonatal Intensive Care Unit if they weren't qualified, right?

"Enchantée," I managed to say even though I was not particularly delighted to meet them.

"Oh, you are American?" Toupee asked.

"Yes."

"That's great!" he said, starting to run his fingers through his hair before quickly pulling out. The tuft of fake blond hair flopped down, hanging awkwardly over the rest of his natural strawberry blond mane. "I love speaking English. English is great. Let's speak English!"

That sounded fun to *one* of us. But I figured I should be nice to the person who would be spending his Saturday night caring for my child.

"Let's see. I'm from St. Louis, M—"

"Louisiana! Yes, I know. St. Louis is a beautiful French city in Louisiana. How do you like it?"

I didn't bother correcting him. "St. Louis is great, though I've lived in Paris for seven years now so..."

"So you prefer Paris. I see. What is your favorite thing about Paris?"

"That's hard to say." It certainly wasn't their Saturday night medical staff. "I love walking down..."

"The streets! Yes, they are lovely. That's my favorite thing about Paris, too. We have so much in common!"

The conversation continued in this fashion until another baby's machine started beeping. What a relief. That makes me sound heartless but I'd come to recognize the various beeps and buzzes of the machines, and knew this one was pretty benign. The baby's feeding tube would need to be refilled within the next five minutes. No biggie. But it got Toupee off my hands.

"Well, me and my toupee are going to take care of that baby. But you let me know if you want to speak any more English!"

Thanks, but I didn't need *him* in order to do that.

I know I shouldn't complain. Our son was receiving excellent care in one of France's best neonatal hospitals. It's just scary to leave your newborn baby with a cigarette and a rug for babysitters.

By Monday, the weirdoes were gone and I had been released from the hospital. While my hospital stay had been enjoyable—surprisingly good food, stellar care, and a baby to show for it all—it was nice to spend the night in my own bed.

That morning, Mika and I scurried around our apartment trying to pack for our long day at the hospital. We ended up forgetting 90% of our stuff at home and brought only our phones and some new clothes for Leo. I was settling quite nicely into the new me—frazzled, clueless, and unprepared.

But at least I had baby clothes! Which is more important than it sounds because with all of Leo's tubes and wires, he had to wear clothes that buttoned up the front. And while France has many fine products to offer, they always fail you when you're looking for something specific. We considered ourselves lucky to have found onesies that snapped up the front after only hitting up four stores.

Overall it was a good day, with our regular hospital staff back on the scene and Leo making great progress. But as new parents with a baby in the NICU, we still spent the whole day worrying about our son and not thinking of ourselves.

I'd forgotten my pain medication, which made sitting in a rocking chair for 14 hours a torturous son-of-a-bitch. And we'd both forgotten to eat. When we finally said a tearful goodbye to Leo (who was asleep and didn't even notice), we stumbled out of the hospital, weak with hunger.

We ended up at the gourmet world-renowned restaurant of McDonald's. I lowered myself onto a chair while Mika took one for the team and waited in the long line. A fresh pounding headache added to my other pain, so I laid my arms on the table and rested my head while waiting for the food.

Screeeeeech.

The telltale sound of a cheap chair scraping across a tile floor was extremely close. As in, it must have come from my table.

I lifted my head to see a young girl sitting across from

me.

Noooooooo!

She had no idea what she'd just done. We were seated at a two-person table, and since I wasn't planning to dine with her while her mom ate with Mika, it meant one of us had to go. And as the adult in the situation, it should probably be me.

I rose from the chair, aching in places I'd never known existed until I'd given birth. I hobbled to a nearby table, praying she wouldn't follow me.

"Hey, how come you switched tables?" Mika asked, arriving with a tray full of calories to feast on.

"Because that stupid little brat over there sat down at our table."

"You mean, that sweet, innocent girl sitting over there by herself? Yeah, she's pretty horrible."

"I hate her," I said, shooting her a look of contempt while stuffing my mouth with fries.

"Question—did you forget to take your pain pills today?"

"Is it that obvious?"

"New plan. Let's make a checklist of everything we need to do each morning, including packing food and taking medicine. Sound good?"

My husband was the best. Not only was a checklist exactly what we needed at that moment, but he had willingly offered to create one. Checklists were my favorite! And maybe it would get us back on track. Be prepared for once.

"She's still a brat. Who sits down next to a total stranger?"

"Um, a nice, friendly girl?"

Yes, I definitely needed to get back on the meds.

11

Your Future in a Crystal Ball

FAITHFULLY TAKING MY PAIN MEDS every morning, I was much better equipped to handle whatever the day threw at me. Mika and I bonded with other parents in the NICU and shared our stories. Nearly everyone had it worse than us—crazier birth story, baby needing to stay in the hospital longer—yet they remained upbeat and positive.

But two families ruined it.

First was this chick who always wore sky high heels and trashy outfits like she was going out clubbing. I'm all for getting your groove back post-partum. It's not like you need to be frumpy in order to care about your fragile little baby. But you don't need to look like a streetwalker, either.

I could set aside her appearance (and write about it later) if she wasn't such a total cow. Instead, she proved to be exactly as much of a cow as she looked.

I discovered this during Rush Hour at the breast-pumping room. Many NICU moms nurse their babies as much as possible while at the hospital, then pump before leaving for the evening, thus creating a mad rush on the two-person pumping room from 6:00 - 7:00 pm. Why couldn't people learn from experience and do it before or after? But no, there was always a long line. And the French are not known for respecting lines.

Add to it the fact that you don't want to stand in the hallway for 15-30 minutes while your episiotomy scar is throbbing. Wouldn't it be much nicer to sit down and wait in your room, holding your baby for those extra precious minutes?

Yes, it would.

And most of the moms adhered to that. There was no official sign-up sheet but you basically loitered around long enough to catch someone's eye, and gave them a nod that said, "I'm next." Then you could return to your room and relax, as much as is possible in the NICU.

But Hell on Heels didn't respect this and totally butted in front of me one night. I had even waited until 7:00 to let the other mothers with more pressing agendas go first. And no, clubbing is not a pressing agenda. Who shows up to a club at 7:00 anyway? She clearly could have waited.

But Hell on Heels waits for no one. As soon as one of the two current occupants exited, she literally pushed past me and slammed the door. I heard the familiar whir of the pump machine before she started jabbering away on her phone.

Oh no she didn't! Cell phones weren't allowed! Hadn't she seen the sign? She was breaking one too many rules. The teacher's pet in me was dying to tattletale on her. How dare she? Not to mention I happened to notice she scored the plush, comfy armchair in Station #1 instead of the rickety folding chair in Station #2. Which meant I'd be stuck with the folding chair whenever the other mom left. Not fair!

Fearful some other inconsiderate jerk would take my spot, I forced myself to wait in the hallway, missing out on time with my baby and wincing in pain.

I tried to keep my cool but honestly I'm just not good at that. I gave her the evil eye, but it didn't do much good through the wooden door. So I resorted to the only alternative—crying.

Yep, that pile of tears in the fluorescent-lit hallway was me. Draped in disposable hospital gown covers, compression stockings peeking out the bottom (we wouldn't want blood clots on top of my other issues), and mismatched hospital booties, I painted one sad picture.

A nurse hurried past me, then did a double-take and backed up. "Madame, are you OK?"

"Oui, I'm fine," I sniffed.

She wasn't convinced. "Are you sure? You can tell me."

"That mean lady butted in front of me for the breast-pumping room and I don't feel good and I want to hold my baby and she's just so mean! And she was talking on her cell phone!"

I was hysterical at this point, tears dripping onto my blue paper gown.

"Oh, I know who you're talking about. We have a real problem with her. Here, let me get you a chair and I'll talk to her when she gets out."

Well *that* made me feel better. Take that, Hell on Heels! Tattletale wins… at least for today.

ക≪

The other family that ticked me off was this pair of gypsies. And I'm not talking the cool fortune-teller kind you see in movies. I'm talking rob-you-in-the-street gypsies.

At first I thought maybe I was judging them too harshly.

"Did you see those people, Mika? I know I looked rough after delivery but, um, I think that lady could use a shower."

"For real. I can still smell them and they walked by five minutes ago."

"Are we being mean?"

"Um, no. This is a sterile hospital environment with babies in critical condition. I saw those two at the front desk and they didn't even wash their hands after they buzzed in."

"Eww! The sign clearly says to wash and sanitize your hands." Welcome back, Tattletale.

"Well, it's not totally their fault. I think they're *Roms* so they might not speak French."

"Roms?" I hadn't heard that term before.

"Yeah, like gypsies. From Romania. That's where a large percentage of the people you see begging in the street come from."

I'd obviously seen the beggars and their different scams during my time in Paris. But I never realized they were all from the same place. Apparently it's a whole operation where each beggar has to report to a boss. They don't even get to keep much of the money they collect, and they live crammed together in caravans, destined to continue this way of life. Makes you kind of feel sorry for them, sitting all day on the same crappy sidewalk, begging for change, only to hand most of it over and then sleep in a crappy caravan. And then wake up to do it again the next day.

"They use babies to garner more sympathy when they beg, and half the time the babies aren't even theirs. A woman with several babies will have to share hers with someone who doesn't have kids. I even heard that they'll buy babies because in the long run it'll pay off with higher begging returns."

OK, I didn't feel sorry for them anymore. My baby was no longer connected to any machines and was ripe for the taking. What if this smelly woman stole Leo and used him to beg on the street?

Mika saw my worried expression and read my mind.

"Don't worry. She's not going to steal our baby." He glanced across the hall at the nurse's station. "There are always nurses around. She wouldn't get away with it."

But he didn't even sound that convinced himself.

As a new mother, one who had to leave her baby in the hospital every night, I was overly sensitive. Understandably so.

That night at home in my nice, clean bed, I tossed and turned as nightmare after nightmare featured the same scenario—returning to the hospital to find my baby gone.

ᖇᖇᖇ

The next day I woke Mika up early so we could go to the hospital and check that Leo was still there. He said I was worrying over nothing, yet I noticed he got ready a little more quickly than usual.

We buzzed into the NICU, dressed in our fashionable disposable gowns, and washed and sanitized our hands. I was itching to see Leo but we had to follow procedure!

When we finally reached our room, I was relieved to see our precious baby was still there. Of course he was. I felt stupid. How could I have been so judgmental?

Later in the day when their scent wafted down the hall, I made sure to have a smile ready for when the couple passed.

The woman grunted and the man averted his eyes. Well, at least I tried.

A short while later, Gypsy Mom entered the breast-pumping room without even bothering to knock. The mother who'd been using the other nursing station dashed out just moments after, and I noticed (hey, there's not much else to look at) that her bottle of milk wasn't quite full. She'd clearly left in a hurry.

Can't say I blame her. The windowless room was only large enough to accommodate two chairs (the prized armchair and the horrible folding chair), two pumps, a water cooler, a trash can, a recycle bin, and a table with the breast-pumping kits. If Gypsy Mom's smell lingered minutes after passing through a hallway, I could only imagine the damage it would cause in a small, enclosed space.

When Gypsy Mom swung open the door after her turn, I saw she had torn the place up. Water was splashed all over the water cooler, yet the pack of plastic cups remained unopened. Had she lapped water directly from the tap?

As my eyes moved around the room, I surveyed even more damage. Each time you start a session, you have to use a brand new pumping kit. It's admittedly bad for the environment but it has to be sterile, and at least you can recycle most of it. Of course Gypsy Mom had messed up the system, throwing the recyclable parts in the trash and the trash on the floor.

Milk was splattered everywhere.

Crumpled paper towels littered the table, though I can't imagine what she'd used them for since the room was a wet disaster. Hurricanes have left rooms looking cleaner.

The cords from the pump were tangled in a huge knot.

But here's what really got me: the cushion from the comfy chair was ON THE FLOOR. She was lucky enough to get the armchair and now she had to contaminate the cushion?

I'm not sure you could do this much damage if you tried. She'd left her mark on every square inch of this tiny room, as if she'd had a checklist of things to destroy and methodically ticked each one off before exiting.

Speaking of checklists, a 15-step process was displayed on one wall of the room, complete with pictures. Fifteen steps is a lot to follow but considering Step 1 is "Wash your hands" it's not like it's rocket science.

Tattletale was furious. We had a sterile environment to maintain! Which this woman had totally compromised.

A nurse came by to retrieve Gypsy Mom's milk (which was in an unlabeled container without a lid—obviously someone didn't follow Steps 13 and 14) and tried in vain to explain the process, which was clearly falling on non-French-speaking ears.

Gypsy Mom just shrugged and ambled down the hall, while the nurse spent the next 30 minutes re-sterilizing the pumping room. Thirty minutes that could have been spent caring for a child in need.

"I wish our room wasn't right across from all the action," I said. "It stresses me out."

"I know. But it's comforting to have the nurse's station so close."

I felt bad for being so judgmental but I was a mama bear now and couldn't help it.

Vindication came a week later. Leo was out of the hospital at last and we were enjoying a stroll down our tree-lined avenue. We crossed a busy intersection, struggling to push the stroller up on the curb before the light changed and without hitting the beggar lady sitting on the corner.

I caught her eye and I'll be damned—Gypsy Mom stared back at me.

"Mika, look," I whispered.

"Oh my god, it's her. You were right!"

Never had it felt so bad to be right. Here I was with my overpriced stroller and the freedom to walk around my posh Parisian neighborhood. And here she was, sitting all day long (that's gotta hurt even if you didn't recently give birth), grimy from the city's pollution. And she didn't even have her baby with her.

Was the baby still in the hospital? Or did she have to give it to someone else? What sort of life would this baby have? After such loving care at the hospital during its first few weeks of life, was it destined to spend the rest of its life in the streets?

I peered down at my baby. It had been a long labor and

a rough eleven days in the NICU. But that was behind us now and we had the whole world in front of us. Relatively speaking, we had it good.

12

"007" Just Sounds Cooler Than "7"

"CRAP, MY ID CARD[7] IS EXPIRED," Mika said one morning as he was about to head out to work.

I was still in my pajamas, enjoying sixteen glorious weeks of maternity leave. Since Leo had come early, I got to spend my full allotment with him, rather than taking the first three weeks off before his birth.

"Can I take care of it for you?" It would be a nice excuse to get some fresh air. The dead heat of August had passed and we were now enjoying milder, but still warm, temperatures. Perfect for a leisurely stroll around the

---

[7] For the Americans in the crowd, let me explain. While we typically use our driver's license as our ID, we might be the only country that does. Europeans have national ID cards, which makes more sense. Not everyone drives, particularly not those who live in big cities. Plus, some countries don't even let you get your driver's license until you're 20, so you need another form of ID before then. I have to admit I agree with the Europeans on this one, even though it means you need an ID *and* a driver's license. Yay, more bureaucracy!

neighborhood.

"I doubt it. I'll go on my lunch break."

Well, I could still take that walk.

I kissed my husband goodbye and began the hour-long process to get Leo and myself ready. I don't know how it takes that long, it just does.

Once packed, I held Leo with my left arm while I locked up the apartment. Then I carefully plodded down the flight of stairs to where our stroller was parked. This was a better solution than carrying the stroller up and down each time, but it was still the most nerve-wracking part of my day.

"You're gonna wanna be careful on those steps," my dad had advised during our weekly phone call the previous Sunday. "I'll never forget dropping you down the stairs when you were a baby."

"What!?! I never heard about that." Or maybe I did but I was too brain damaged to remember.

"Then I probably shouldn't tell you, but I will. It was in our house out in Colorado. It had these stupid carpeted stairs and I was wearing socks but no shoes and somehow I slipped. You flew out of my arms and rolled down the steps like a corn cob. You were OK, but I nearly had a heart attack."

I nearly had a heart attack just listening to the story.

"So, let me give you some advice. Never walk down carpeted stairs in socks."

"But my stairs don't have carpet and they're outside the apartment so I'm always wearing shoes."

"You still need to be careful."

"OK, so to sum up, your advice is 'Be careful on stairs.' Got it."

I looked down at my little corn cob as I descended at a snail's pace. I was in no hurry.

Once he was safely buckled in—I triple checked—I now had get out to the street. This was harder than it sounds. At the end of the stairwell was a door that opened inward. I was never able to pass through it without bumping the stroller against the door a hundred times. Which subsequently attracted the attention of the kindly concierge who lived across the courtyard from our stairwell.

"Bonjour, Madame Lesage! Let me help."

She rushed out of her apartment, not even bothering to close her door, and skipped across the cobbled courtyard to assist me. Her dark dreadlocks were secured in a high pony tail, and her colorful sundress flowed in the breeze.

She held the door as I pushed the stroller out, then came around to the front of the stroller, lifted it up, and motioned for me to pick up the back.

"We don't want to jostle that beautiful baby's brains by wheeling him over the stones. You come get me anytime and I will help. I want only the best for Leandro. He brings so much joy to this building."

Leandro? Well, close enough to Leonardo. I wasn't about to correct someone who had been so nice.

She opened the front door of the building and held it as I passed.

"Bonne journée! And don't forget to buzz me when you return and I'll help you."

"Merci," I said. She was too kind!

I stopped for coffee and orange juice at the corner café, snagging a shaded spot on the terrace. A fountain bubbled in the center of the roundabout, and people passed at an easy pace. Normally I'd be working this time of day, but now I got to enjoy mid-morning Parisian life.

A mother window-shopped as her young daughter, about two years old, ran toward us. The girl squealed when she saw Leo in his stroller.

"Maman!" she shouted back to her mother. "Bébé!" She toddled up and peeked in at my sleeping baby.

"Sorry," the mother said with a smile. "She loves

babies."

"No problem!" How adorable was that? A baby calling another baby "bébé." I guess to a two-year-old a newborn does seem pretty young.

I finished my beverages then headed home. It would be time to feed Leo soon—it always was. As I arrived back to 64 Boulevard Descartes, I started to punch in the door code. Then I remembered that the concierge said to buzz her. Should I? I couldn't possibly disrupt her every time I came and went—that was way beyond her job description. Plus I hated asking for help if I could handle it myself.

I re-entered the code, then quietly pushed open the heavy wooden door. I eased the stroller past, then gently closed the door behind me.

Now for the cobblestones. I had about 50 feet of bumpy path to cover. I lifted the handles of the stroller, raising the hind wheels off the ground, and crept as quietly as possible over the stones. I'd just made it to the door of our stairwell when her voice rang out behind me.

"Madame Lesage!"

Busted.

"Look who's back! Let me see those big beautiful eyes, Leandro." She cooed at him while he started blankly back. "And those lashes! I've never seen such long lashes on a baby! You puttin' mascara on that boy?"

"Isn't it incredible? His lashes are longer than mine!"

"Gorgeous baby. Now, let me help you into your apartment," she said, heading for the stairs. "Why didn't you buzz me? I want the best for Leandro, so please let me help."

I wanted the best for "Leandro" too, so I gave in. She held open the door and let me pass, then waited as I unbuckled Leo from his stroller. As we slowly mounted the stairs, she took my keys and opened my front door, pushing it wide for us to enter.

"Bonne journée, Madame. And don't forget—I'm here

for you and Leandro."

⚜

"I don't know what I'm going to do about our concierge," I said to Mika that night over dinner. "She's too nice."

"Wow, that sounds horrible." He winked.

"Well, I mean, c'mon! I can't ask her to help every time I go out, but she busted me when I tried to sneak in behind her back. Maybe I'll stay home forever. Or at least run all my errands on the same trip so that I minimize how much I bother her."

"You might be overthinking it. You could just let her help you."

"We'll see. Anyway, how did it go at lunch, for renewing your ID?"

"Fine. The line was long, as expected, but everything should be in order. I need to go back in two weeks to pick it up."

Knowing French administration, I doubted it would be that easy. Then again, he was one of 65 million French people who had to renew their IDs. Surely they'd ironed out the process by now.

⚜

"Check this out," Mika said two weeks later sliding his new ID card across the table.

"Ooh, shiny! Congrats. That was easier than I thought it would be."

"Take a closer look."

I peered at the tiny print and closely read each line. Seemed fine to me. Oh wait. "04 Boulevard Descartes? Ha! No way."

"I guess my '6' looked like a '0' on the form," Mika

said, taking the blame for something he shouldn't have.

"Um, no. First of all, when are these people going to stop hand writing stuff and start using computers? It's 2012! Second, who puts a zero in front of their address? Are you James Bond? 'Hi, I'm 0-Mika and I live at 04 Boulevard Descartes.' Imbeciles!"

"Yep. Now I have to go back and resubmit the paperwork."

"You didn't do that when you picked up the card?"

He gave me a look that said, "What do you think?"

"Ah, let me guess," I said. "They were a few minutes away from going on lunch break so they asked you to come back tomorrow."

"You got it!"

"So you need to resubmit the paperwork then go back again to pick up the card. Four trips total."

"If I'm lucky."

"Good luck, Bond. James Bond."

13

Stars and Stripes

A COMMON SIDE EFFECT OF PREGNANCY, which continues even after the baby is born, is a concept called "baby brain." That's a nice way of saying "you've lost your mind." Coupled with living in a French-speaking country, I functioned at a cerebral level slightly below an amoeba.

Though the end of a hot, humid summer was drawing near, my skin was unusually dry. So I loaded Leo into the stroller, snuck past the concierge, and headed out to buy lotion.

The perfumed shop was overwhelming.

Crème mains, soins de mains, lait de savon, huiles, gels, creams, lotions, and potions. Strawberry, almond, vanilla, mint. Elegant bottles, functional bottles.

I selected a bottle of *lait de savon*. Since *lait* means "milk," I figured my hands would be smooth and silky in no time. I faithfully used my *lait de savon* after each hand-washing, determined to rid myself of my zombie claws and return to the land of the living.

After a few days, my skin was worse than ever. Dry and cracked. White flakes blew off in the breeze, as if my hands had dandruff.

"This lotion sucks, Mika! And it wasn't even that cheap. What the heck?" We had brushed our teeth and were about to settle in bed to catch a few hours of sleep before Leo woke up for yet another feeding.

"Which lotion?"

"This stupid *lait de savon*."

He started to laugh but stopped when he saw my face. "Sorry, but *lait de savon* is soap."

"But…" Oh. OK. That made sense now. I'd been so focused on the *lait* part that I'd ignored the *savon* part, *savon* being the French word for "soap." I peeked down at my hands and had to laugh. "I've been rubbing soap on my hands for the past three days? Awesome."

The fun didn't stop there. One day I poured milk into my water glass instead of my coffee mug. And then stared at it for a full minute before I could figure out what was wrong with that picture.

Another day I went to the ATM and couldn't remember my PIN, even though I'd used my card the day before.

The most peculiar thing was when I began using homophones uncontrollably. I'd type a text message saying "Weighting at doctor's office, hope their not running two late." Granted, half the world writes (rights?) texts worse than that. But as a writer, I should have caught (cot?) those mistakes.

Good thing I still had plenty of maternity leave remaining before going back to work. My brain was definitely not ready.

∾⸲

My next big "project"—everything seemed like a big

deal to my overtired little brain—was to declare Leo as a U.S. citizen and get him a passport.

U.S. passports require different sized photos than French ones, which makes this the one case where the U.S. is more difficult than France. Instead of popping into one of the numerous photo booths around town, you have to find one of the few shops that offer special (read: overpriced) American passport photos.

Lucky for us, one such place was right down the street. Certain we would encounter difficulties, I held off until my mom came to visit.

On a bright, sunny morning, Mom, Mika, and I loaded Leo into the stroller and exited our building. At least the concierge didn't try to help.

"Bonjour," the kind, round-faced owner of the photo shop greeted us. "How can I help you?"

"Bonjour, we'd like an American passport photo for this little guy," I said, pointing to my lump of a baby, drooling in his sleep.

"Sure, no problem! His eyes need to be open for the photo, though, so do you want to come back when he's awake?"

Had he never met a newborn before?

"Well, since he's only a few weeks old, he pretty much sleeps all the time. And our appointment at the embassy is tomorrow, so we kind of have to do it now."

"OK, then! Let's see what we can do!"

I unbuckled Rip Van Winkle and carried him over to the swiveling stool in the portrait studio. How on earth was this going to work?

Judging by the shop owner's expression, I could tell he was asking himself the same question.

"Let's see if you can prop him up, and if your hand shows I'll Photoshop it out."

I did as I was told, but Leo was still out like a light. His head slumped down and you couldn't even see his face.

"Mika, let's switch," I suggested.

Mika held our son while my mom and I shouted "Leo! Leo!" to wake him up. With each shout, he would jerk his head up, open his eyes, and then slump back to sleep.

The photographer had been clicking away the whole time.

"Did you get any good shots?"

"Nope, he falls back asleep too quickly. His eyes are closed in every one."

Crap. At least he didn't look like a serial killer, which is how all my passport photos turn out. You're not supposed to smile but I don't know how to hold a serious expression without looking like I want you dead.

"I have an idea," the photographer said. "Here, you take the camera and I'll take the baby. When I say 'click' you push this button here," he said, indicating a button on his fancy camera that I probably wouldn't have found on my own.

He managed to prop Leo's head up with his hand so that at least Leo was facing the camera. Mika and Mom shouted Leo's name, and I clicked when the photographer said "click." I felt cool, like a professional shooting at Paris Fashion Week. Except my model was a droopy pile of baby with drool running down his chin.

The bell on the shop's door jingled as a customer entered. "Bonjour! Um, is this a bad time?"

We turned to the new arrival then looked back at the scene. It must have seemed hilarious. A customer holding the camera while the photographer clutched the back of a sleeping baby's shirt in a crouched position behind the stool, while the two other adults in the room were shouting.

"Bonjour, I'll be right with you, sir," the patient shop owner said, gently placing Leo in Mom's arms while coming over to review the shots I captured. "Great, one of these should work. Can you come back in a few hours? I'll have them printed up by then."

We walked out of the store, the four of us exhausted from the ordeal.

"I think you ended up with some nice shots," Mom said. "My grandbaby is going to have the cutest passport photo ever!"

"Good, since it will last him for five years. Which is funny, if you think about it. They insist that his eyes be open yet they'll let you use a newborn photo until they're five years old? Seems like it'd be easier to recognize a baby with their eyes closed than to compare a photo against a child who's five years older in real life."

I could picture the border control officer five years down the road. "Hrm, something's different. Is it his hair? His head isn't as cone-shaped. I'm not sure this is the same kid. Oh wait. The eyes. They're the same. You're good to go," he'd say, stamping the passport and sending us on our way.

"And another thing," I added, not done analyzing this scenario to death. "His eyes are blue now but they're likely to change as he gets older. Using the eyes as a gauge doesn't even make sense."

"Well, I'm not arguing," Mika said. "I'm just happy we're done with that for another five years."

The next day, pictures of my photogenic little model in hand and mounds of paperwork filled out, our quartet set off for the embassy to score dual citizenship for my French *bébé*.

We rode the Métro to Concorde and emerged at street-level to the busiest intersection in Paris. Streets shoot off at every angle, taking you to the beautiful church of Madeleine to the north, the famous Champs-Élysées and Arc de Triomphe to the west, and to the place where my son would obtain American citizenship if I would stop sightseeing like a tourist and start watching where I pushed my stroller.

"I remember this place!" My mom stopped as she fished her camera out of her purse. "Wasn't your wedding reception right down that road? Ooh, and isn't that the Tuileries Gardens across the street?"

See where I get it from?

She snapped a few quick photos before we crossed the road to the grand building that housed the U.S. Embassy.

౨◆౨

Ding! Our ticket number displayed on the overhead monitor, with "18" noted next to it, indicating which *guichet* to go to. I carried Leo while my mom brought the paperwork.

"Hello! You're here to declare citizenship for Leonardo Quentin Lesage, correct? Which one of you is the mother?"

Mom and I were both flattered. Mom, because it implied she looked young enough to have a newborn (she does look extremely young for her age) and me because it implied I was so thin I couldn't possibly have given birth a few weeks ago (I totally looked like I had given birth a few weeks ago).

"I am," I managed to sputter out.

"Great. I need you to hold up that right hand and swear by your statement."

"My hand or my baby's?"

"Yours, ma'am," he said, without giving me the stupid look I deserved. "Do you swear that all information declared on this form is true?"

"Yes."

"And some other super official bureaucratic mumbo jumbo?"

"Yes."

"Then by the authority of the U.S. Government I declare Leonardo Quentin Lesage an American citizen."

A few people seated behind us clapped.

"Here's your flag," the man said, sliding a miniature American flag under the glass barrier. "Congratulations."

Chills of pride ran down my spine. My son was now an American! A sleeping, drooling American who needed a diaper change.

14

Class out the Ass

MATERNITY LEAVE SUITED ME WELL. I got to spend tons of time with my baby, I snuck in naps wherever possible, and I enjoyed peeking through windows of swanky Parisian boutiques as I pushed my bundle of joy in his stroller.

I'd get Leo ready, dressing him in one of the hundreds of adorable, classy French outfits friends and family had showered us with. Then I'd top it off with a spritz of—I kid you not—baby cologne. Not that he needed it since he had that sweet baby smell, but how could I resist the extravagance of Eau de Bébé? The French really are an interesting breed.

One day I loaded him in the Baby Bjorn and hopped on the Métro to BHV, a behemoth of a department store situated in my favorite *quartier*, the Marais.

It's an upscale place, though not quite as nice as their prices would have you believe. And no matter how efficient I am, I always get lost and end up hot and sweaty and scrambling for the nearest exit.

But I needed a new Brita pitcher and this was the only store nearby that sold them. I would have been better off ordering online, but then I would miss out on the city's charm. Heh.

Checking out a store directory while Leo slept against my chest, I located the housewares department on the sixth floor. I took the escalators, one by one, up six stories, then weaved through displays of 50-euro coffee mugs and escargot plates until I found the water filtration section. There, I was met with the typical French pricing system: wacky colors are the cheapest, semi-normal colors cost 15% more, and then only if you're lucky will you find neutral colors—and for this you pay a 25% premium.

Why couldn't they have a clear one or a white one? Who wants a fuchsia or blood-red water pitcher? Heck, I'd even settle for blue. But alas, I had to go for green, and pay 15% more for the privilege. I have no idea what costs 15% more about a green one but it was worth it to not have my water pitcher blind me every time I opened the fridge.

Now, I just needed to check out. This was something that should be easy but never was at BHV. Mika and I had created a wedding registry there and still had some credit left on our store card. That part was quite advanced for France—gift givers have the option of selecting an item from your online registry and "sending" it to you, but in fact it just puts money on your card. That way you can go back later and get something else if you change your mind.

It also means that instead of having the gift conveniently delivered to your house, you have to make a trip to their maze of a store and lug it home yourself. Hrm, maybe it's not as convenient as I thought.

But we found it handy because we hadn't used up our credit and so now anytime we wanted to buy something, it was free.

The only glitch? The magnetic strip on the card didn't work. The first time I'd made a purchase I waited in the long check-out line only to have our card embarrassingly declined.

"You'll have to go to customer service," the cashier said. "Next!"

"Pardon me, where's customer service?" I'd asked. But she had already moved on to the next customer. Where was this efficiency when I'd been waiting in line?

Winding through the increasingly warm store, I'd found the customer service counter, waited in another long line, and handed over my card. The cashier swiped it, no problem.

"But it didn't work for the other cashier! That's weird," I'd said.

"Yeah, sometimes these cards work, sometimes they don't." He shrugged, clearly not caring about my wasted thirty minutes.

"So next time should I come directly here?"

"No. You're not allowed to do that. Try it first at the regular cash registers and then come here if it doesn't work."

That sounded like a colossal waste of time. Plus, how would they know if I'd tried a regular check-out lane first?

Now, Brita pitcher in hand, I went straight to the customer service counter. Little Miss Tattletale had become a full-blown rebel.

"Bonjour, Madame. How can I help you?"

"Bonjour. I tried to pay for this at that cash register," I said, vaguely pointing behind me, "but my card didn't work so they sent me here. There's a problem with the magnetic strip."

"Which cash register?"

My face reddened. Was I getting busted? For *this*?

"The one over there," I said, indicating a large enough area with the circular motion of my finger that it surely had to contain a check-out. I turned back to him, ready to play chicken.

I could tell he didn't believe me, but apathy won out. He shrugged, then punched my card's 16-digit code into his computer.

"Merci, Madame. Bonne journée," he said, shoving my gaudy pitcher into a bag and sending me on my way.

Victory!

I headed to the elevator, not having the patience to descend six floors of escalators one by one. The button was already lit, likely having been pressed by the perfectly coiffed elderly woman waiting in front of the doors. Hopefully the elevator would arrive soon. The heat of the store, combined with my white lie and a sleeping baby on my chest, had made me dizzy. I needed to get out of there.

Right then, Leo woke up just long enough to smile and release a sonic boom of a fart, one that was both loud and long. And stinky. Satisfied with his work, he snuggled contentedly against me and fell back asleep.

The woman stared at me with that "Oh my" expression old ladies have, you know, the one where they place their hand on their chest and act like they've never heard a fart before.

Yeah, I really needed to get out of there.

The elevator dinged and the three of us piled in, the rank odor following us.

At least by now I'd mastered how to do the French shrug of apathy.

15

General Lesage

MUCH AS I ENJOYED MY TIME OFF WORK, I was going to have to return. Which meant we needed to figure out our childcare situation.

Growing up, my brother, Stephen, and I went to afterschool daycare since my parents were divorced and my mom worked full-time. Nowadays you hear horror stories about daycare and I see on mommy forums what a bad mom you are if you do something as heinous as send your kids to daycare, but we absolutely loved it.

They had loads more books and games and activities than we had at home. Snack time was awesome because someone else cleaned up after you. Plus, as I was one of the older kids, I was leader of the pack. I can't even tell you how many times I made the kids be my audience while I re-enacted dance scenes from Dirty Dancing. Did I ever tell you I was cool?

Several childcare options are available in Paris. You can hire a nanny, and if you select one from the government's approved list and pay above-the-table, then you can qualify for government subsidies. The native French-speakers get snatched up right away, and you'll rarely find an English-speaker on the list. I'm sure the remaining nannies are fine—they are state-approved after all—but I didn't want my son getting confused by yet another accent in our already bilingual household.

You can hire an *au pair* but you are expected to provide room and board. Unless she wanted to sleep in the same bed with Mika and me (which was in the same room as Leo's crib) that wouldn't work. Also, a lot of the girls I met in bars from my partying days were *au pairs*. Not to be the pot calling the kettle black but, um, I'm not sure I want my child's caregiver to be dancing on bars in her spare time. I'm the only person allowed to shake my booty to George Michael and then wipe my son's booty the next day.

Then you have various forms of daycare, one being a *familial* where parents are expected to contribute a few hours. I didn't see how that could work, considering the whole reason I needed daycare was because I'd be going back to work full-time.

And finally you have the *crèche*, which is a state-run daycare that's almost like school. It's affordable and clean, and therefore extremely sought after. Only about one in ten applicants gets in. You can apply as early as the sixth month of pregnancy, and thankfully Mika had submitted our application at six months to the day. Then you just had to pray to the daycare gods and wait to see if you got accepted.

"You know, I go back to work in a few weeks. I guess we can assume we didn't get accepted to the *crèche*?" I said to Mika over dinner one night.

"That sucks! We submitted before the deadline. And I followed up numerous times. Plus we had a CV for Leo. They totally should have picked us!"

In an attempt to give ourselves a leg up on the

competition, Mika submitted a mini résumé for Leo with his last follow-up letter. It was the cutest thing I'd ever seen, highlighting his experiences, education, and interests. Leo's main hobbies were observing the world from his stroller and immersing himself in French and American culture. He was three months old.

"I guess we need to look for a nanny," I said. "I don't even know how to do that."

"The city hall has a monthly informational meeting for parents," Mika said. "I'll dig up the details and maybe you can go?"

Ugh. Of course I would go and I was sure we'd find a decent nanny. It's just that we really wanted the *crèche*. Not only did we think it would be a better environment for our bilingual child, it cost about half the price.

Not known for my patience, the wait to find out was killing me. And I was pretty sure we wouldn't get accepted anyway. Too bad I couldn't barge into City Hall, grab someone by the tie, and demand it. Not that I would ever do that.

❧

In my high school Advanced Placement Calculus class, I essentially did just that. We were nearing the end of the school year and to prep for the AP exam, Dr. Buss, the best teacher of all time, had us practice integration for a week straight.

For this math nerd, it was a dream come true.

Not only was it a full week of my favorite type of math but he turned it into a competition. I was practically salivating.

Each day we'd arrive to class to see several problems already chalked onto the board. Students would volunteer to complete different parts of the problem and once it had been solved, Cody a shy, freckled classmate of mine, would draw a star after the name of whoever he felt had contributed the most.

The goal was to obtain five stars by the end of the week so that you could be a Five-Star General, the army's highest rank. But with 22 students and only eight problems per day, it would be impossible for every student to attain five stars. I'd have to work for it.

I faithfully raised my hand for each problem but Cody would only call on me if no one else had raised their hand. And if anyone else had worked on the problem, he would always assign the star to the other person.

What was his problem? Didn't he see that I needed to be a Five-Star General?

Actually, I could think of a few reasons he might not have liked me.

Throughout my high school career, I tried out various personas. I was always a nerd—that couldn't be changed. I participated in after school math contests for extra credit and was enrolled in all honors classes.

But I also went through a grunge-turned-riot-grrrl phase where Kurt Cobain and Courtney Love were my biggest idols. I won't say I partied (because my mom is reading this and I was way too young) but I will admit I was a bit of an ass. I wore sunglasses in the school hallways. I wore babydoll dresses and Mary Jane patent leather heels, even in the dead cold of winter. I thought I was pretty cool.

I also had a mean streak for a brief spell. I was sassy (I made fashion police tickets and handed them out to offenders) and I'm ashamed to say I made fun of people who didn't deserve it. I don't specifically remember making fun of Cody but as I said, I was an ass, so it was entirely possible.

But in the final months of my senior year, while my peers were slacking off and skipping class, I was determined to pull in the highest grades possible before heading off to college.

Though the honor of Five-Star General couldn't be heralded on a college application, it still represented who I wanted to be.

I had to have it.

On the final day of Integration Week, I was tied with three other people for Four-Star General. I studiously raised my hand and Cody routinely ignored me. Timid Cody had transformed into a pompous tyrant.

The last problem of the week was a doozy but I knew how to solve it. I stretched my hand in the air saying "Ooh, ooh!" and as no one else had any suggestions (or cared), he had no choice but to call on me.

"I suggest repeated application of integration by parts." The fifth star was within reach! I marched up to the chalkboard and worked that bad boy to the end.

Well, almost the end. Somehow I'd messed up one of the iterations. I was so close but just couldn't figure out what I'd done wrong. The star was slipping from my grasp.

I turned back to see Cody smirking, then noticed a raised hand. Crap! Carrie Chang was going to solve my problem and get my star!

She fixed one minor error and the problem was complete.

"Correct!" Dr. Buss announced. Now for the moment of judgment. "Cody, to whom do you award the star?"

"Carrie, of course. She's the one who solved the problem."

"OK then," Dr. Buss said as he walked over to the chalkboard on the side of the room where the stars were being tracked. He added a fifth star next to Carrie's name. I couldn't believe it. I'd failed.

"Great work everyone, I'm really–"

"Excuse me, Dr. Buss," I interrupted. "But I'm going to have to disagree."

I rose from my seat and walked to the chalkboard as I

started an impromptu speech. "For some reason, Cody doesn't like me. And that's his right. But we all know that I did 95% of the work on that problem. No offense to Carrie, but that star should be mine." I erased her star and drew one next to my name, then turned defiantly back to the classroom. "Does anyone have a problem with that?"

The class was silent, some students' faces showing amusement, the rest counting down the minutes until the weekend.

"Well then, we have our Five-Star General. Congratulations, Vicki," Dr. Buss said.

I did it! I had ruthlessly commandeered an entire class (and teacher) for a completely pointless goal that only I cared about. I would make a great general!

༄

Back in Paris, that bravado wouldn't help in my current situation. I slid Leo into the baby carrier and rubbed his mop of hair before heading out to the nanny meeting. It would be OK. Nannies were qualified caregivers and Leo would be fine. Even if it meant we'd go broke.

I descended the stairs and spotted the concierge watering the plants in the courtyard.

"Bonjour Madame Lesage! How are you and Leandro doing today?"

"We're great. We're on our way to a meeting about finding a nanny."

"Good luck! Oh, hold on. I have a piece of mail for you."

One of a concierge's jobs is to deliver the mail to each apartment. I've never understood why the mailman can't do that. Like, couldn't they install mailboxes at the front of the building and then the postman slips the letters into each one? Even buildings that do have mailboxes still require the concierge to sort and deliver the mail to each box. It's weird.

I tilted my face to the warm sunlight while shielding Leo's head from the harmful rays. What a beautiful fall day.

"Here you go, Madame Lesage," the concierge said as she handed me a letter. It was from City Hall. Interesting.

"Bonne journée," I shouted over my shoulder as I tore open the envelope.

I couldn't believe my eyes. We'd been accepted into the *crèche*!

It was excellent news, plus now I could skip the stupid meeting. I had my whole afternoon free. I decided to go for a coffee and called Mika on the way.

"Guess what?" I said.

"Leo is the cutest baby in the world."

"Yes. But also, we got into the *crèche*! We got the letter in the mail as I was literally on my way to the nanny meeting."

"That's awesome! You know, if you ever wrote a book about that, no one would believe it happened that way."

"Ha, I know. Especially since nothing ever seems to go smoothly for me with French administration."

I didn't need to be a Five-Star General, or take anything by force, to get what I wanted. I just needed a little luck and a cute résumé.

16

The Red Card

WE WERE THRILLED to get accepted into the *crèche*. Not only did it solve our childcare predicament, it was also easy on the wallet.

I've heard that some people pay upwards of $2,000 per month in the U.S. for childcare, whereas our monthly rate was in the 400-500 euro range.

That said, I was totally against the system.

The city hall for each *arrondissement* reviews the applications and has some sort of secret criteria for determining who they accept. Payment for the *crèche*—which might I remind you is the same service for each child—is based on the parents' salary. To ensure they have a fair representation of the people living in the *arrondissement* while still having enough funds to run the *crèche*, they have quotas of low-income, middle-income, and higher-income families to accept.

Mika and I didn't rake in the dough (if we did, I'd live in an apartment where my knees didn't touch the bathroom door when using the toilet) but since we were a double-income household I do think that played a part into us getting accepted.

I know I shouldn't look a gift horse in the mouth (except that's exactly the type of thing I do), but, um, doesn't this sound like communism?

Or if we want to bring it down a notch it at least bears resemblance to Robin Hood. Take from the rich to give to the poor. Make the people who earn more pay more so that the people who can't afford it receive the same benefits.

Food, health care, education—I can see these being necessities that we should all chip in on for the greater good. But child care seems to sit slightly more on the optional side of the scale. Especially since there are many options available other than the prestigious *crèche*.

But as a stranger in a strange land, I knew I should keep my mouth shut and be happy for what I had. After all, the French health care system was amazing and croissants were cheap. You just can't compare it to the U.S. Or Iron Curtain-Era U.S.S.R.

∽∾

Before dropping your little cabbage (as they say in French) off at the *crèche* and running along your merry way, they offer a one-week "adaptation" period. This is as much for the parents as the babies, I realized.

On the first day, you leave your baby in the nursery to get acquainted while you enjoy coffee and pastries during a casual talk with the *directrice* of the *crèche* and other new parents.

"Welcome, everyone!" Amélie, a tall, olive-skinned beauty with chestnut hair greeted us. She was probably a *sage-femme* in a former life.

"I am the *directrice* of the *crèche*. I was formerly a NICU nurse and love working with kids."

See? I was close.

"Please sit back, relax, and help yourself to the cookies. Our chef baked them this morning just for you."

They had a chef? At the daycare?

The smell of chocolate chip cookies filled the room. I wanted to stuff about eight of them in my face. But they were sitting on the other end of the table and none of the skinny French ladies was making a move. I thought about asking Mika to do it for me, but since he was the only guy present, he was acting unusually shy.

"Let's go around the room and get acquainted."

No! Let's pass the cookies!

One by one, the moms introduced themselves. A disheveled but attractive lady had a three-year-old son and a pair of six-month-old twins, a boy and a girl. Yowza. And I thought I was busy with just my one poop-and-spit-up machine.

The woman next to her also had a three-year-old and a pair of twins, a boy and a girl. What are the chances?

The next lady told us, no less than five times, that she had a daughter who was two years, two weeks old and that she had breastfed her for two years and two weeks. So… did she stop today? Is she still nursing? Does she update her speech each day? Do I care? Just pass the damn cookies!

Screw it. I reached for the plate and grabbed two napkins and four cookies, splitting my spoils with Mika. Hell yeah, those were good.

When my turn came around, I wiped the crumbs from my lips and said, "Bonjour, I'm American and my husband here is French. Our son is three months old." At the word "American" everyone nodded, as if that explained the cookie-snatching. I let Mika take over so I could finish stuffing my face.

The rest of the meeting was even more boring than the

introductions. Tough crowd. Were all the parents so stiff?

ை௸

The next day I was to bring Leo to his classroom and stay with him for a few hours. That way he and I would both feel at ease. I recognized a few of the parents from the previous day's coffee break but none of them was any friendlier.

Fortunately, the teachers were amazing. You could tell they loved babies and had chosen the perfect career.

"Maman de Leonardo! Come sit next to me," a boisterous woman with tousled graying hair said. "Let's find a toy for Leonardo to play with while you fill me in on who he is and what his interests are."

I propped him in my lap and she handed him a fake wedge of Brie to play with. Scattered around the play mat was an assortment of French picnic staples: baguettes, grapes, and various other cheeses. Even the plastic food was gourmet here!

"My name is Marceline. And you're American, your husband is French, and your son's name is Italian. Is your family Italian?"

"My grandfather's side is from Sicily and my husband's grandfather's side is from the boot heel."

"Ah, yes, so that's why I detect a petite Italian accent. Fabulous! Leonardo will grow up to be trilingual."

"Oh no, I don't–"

"So, tell me more about Leonardo."

I wanted to start with "his mom doesn't actually speak Italian" but I sensed I was never going to be able to correct that in her mind. Between our concierge calling him Leandro and Marceline thinking I spoke Italian, I sure had a lot of misperceptions to keep track of.

"Leo likes to observe the world around him and pretty much never stops moving. Even when he's seated, he tends to do the 'bicycle' with his legs." As if to prove my point, he started pedaling the air, while still maintaining a kung-fu grip on his Brie.

"Good, good. What else?"

Should I send her the link to his online dating profile? He was three months old! He liked to eat, sleep, and poop, sometimes all at once.

"He enjoys my singing, which makes him the one person on the planet to do so, and he likes snuggling."

I was running out of things to say.

"Great! Let me run you through what a typical day here will be like for Leonardo."

She outlined a program that was relaxed yet structured. Sounded like baby school! I felt so happy Leo would be a part of this, even if it was run by a bunch of card-carrying commies.

"In the beginning, the babies will drink bottles at mealtimes. As you introduce new foods at home, let us know and we will do the same here. Each Monday, Chef posts the menu for the week. You can check the meal plan to ensure you don't serve the same dish for dinner."

Uh, no worries there. I'm pretty sure they don't serve hot dogs and mac and cheese at the *crèche*. This place was so much classier than me I was almost intimidated. Except that Marceline was so darn friendly.

"And you'll need to bring a few spare changes of clothes in case of a diaper blow-out or spit-up. We'll do our best to match the spare clothes with the rest of his outfit."

Glad they had the important bases covered.

"Any questions?"

No, other than, could I go here too? I wanted to play and have nap time and eat fancy meals and have someone dress me. This place was wonderful!

"No, I think that about does it."

"Perfect. We look forward to welcoming Leonardo to our *crèche*. We'll see you tomorrow!"

17

Makin' Bacon

ONCE MOMMY AND LEO WERE COMFORTABLE with the *crèche* arrangement, I had to go back to work.

This meant taking the Métro *sans bébé* for the first time in ages. No Baby Bjorn or stroller to deal with, just me and a book. Ah, time to relax.

The train pulled in to Gare de Lyon, the automatic doors opened, and I hopped on. Checking to the left then right, I didn't see any open seats. Bummer, since I had 17 stops ahead of me. But as I was no longer pregnant, I didn't have an excuse to ask for someone's seat.

"Madame, would you like to sit down?" a middle-aged man offered.

Um, I did want to sit down but why was he offering? He glanced at my belly and then stood up. Well, since he was already up I might as well take the seat before someone else did.

"Merci, monsieur," I said as my cheeks reddened. Here I thought I'd done such a good job of losing the baby weight and now I had a guy offering me his seat.

How embarrassing.

I stuck my belly out until he got off the Métro, which was thankfully only a few stops later. Even though he was the one who'd made the presumption, I didn't want him to be embarrassed by realizing I wasn't pregnant.

You may think that was a lot of work to go through to avoid hurting a total stranger's feelings, but that wasn't the first time.

❧

My first summer in Paris was a hot one. I usually wore jeans or a long skirt to cover up my pale, freckly legs and then made up for it by wearing a tank top or loose, flowing shirt.

On July 14, France's Independence Day, I'd met up with some friends to watch fireworks at the Eiffel Tower. I was dressed in my uniform—jeans and a tank top—but in hindsight this particular top had a maternity feel to it. It was fitted through the chest and loose below. Perfect for letting the July breeze in.

The fireworks show was amazing but by the time it finished I was sweltering. I bid my friends adieu and headed to the Métro. I could have walked but I thought the Métro would be quicker.

However, approximately 15 million other people had the same idea. The platform was jam-packed and so was each train that pulled in to the station. The automatic doors would open but there was no room to get on. And there were so many people pushing behind me that I couldn't exit the station and walk home if I wanted to. I was stuck.

About twenty minutes later, a train with a little wiggle room entered the station. Whew, finally.

I boarded and leaned against one of the seats that flips up and down, not daring to sit on it when the train was that full. However, I felt faint and people were pushing against me from all directions. It would have been nice to sit but I resisted. I didn't want to be *that* jerk.

The buzzer sounded, indicating the doors would be closing. That normally means "if you're near the door, pull all your limbs in and if you're on the platform wait for the next train." But much like the jerkwads who run yellow lights, you'll always have one douchebag who pushes his way on at the last second, instigating a round of human dominoes.

Which resulted in me getting elbowed in the belly.

Which caused me to lean back over the seat in reaction.

Which pushed my belly out, making me look pregnant. In a shirt that already resembled the latest in maternity wear.

"Watch out, everyone," a petite, Asian lady shouted. "You're crushing this poor pregnant woman."

How horrible that this throng of sweaty people was crushing an innocent pregnant woman! Except that woman was me and I wasn't pregnant.

"No, no, I'm not–"

"Yes, you *are* being crushed. Everyone move and let her sit down!" This lady was tiny but effective. The crowd parted and I was able to straighten my back and stand up.

"I meant I'm not–"

"Don't protest, it's your right to sit. Here," she said, pushing down the flippy seat and gently guiding me into it.

After all the hubbub, I really had no choice but to go with it. I only had to endure three more stops, so I did what I had to—I stuck my belly out as far as it would go, patted it gently, and smiled my thanks to everyone.

When we arrived at my station, I made a big show of standing up, placing one hand on my lower back for support.

"Merci, tout le monde," I said as I stepped into the slightly cooler air. I kept up the charade until the train left the station. Then I vowed to go on a diet.

❦

On the Métro to work my first day back, I was similarly embarrassed and vowed to go on another diet. But I would enjoy my seat while it lasted.

The train pulled into Esplanade de la Défense and I made my way to the office. First day back. Was I ready?

I spent the first hour giving the *bises* (cheek kisses) to all fifty of my co-workers, then grabbed a cup of coffee and caught up on gossip.

By the time I returned to my desk and downloaded my 2,345 emails, it was lunch time.

"Do you want to go to Subway? One just opened down the street." My co-worker, Marie, was about as tall, beautiful, and French as they come. She was also fluent in English and loved America.

"Sure!" It might be easier to stick to my diet with a sandwich than typical French fare.

Subway in France is way better than in the U.S. Their standards are high and the meats and veggies are always fresh.

However, as the concept is still relatively new here, the French public has no clue what they're doing. Used to simple, pre-made baguette sandwiches, dressed with one slice of ham, one slice of cheese, and five pounds of butter, they've never had to make a decision in their lives. Far from the comfort of their neighborhood *boulangerie*, these clowns make a one-minute transaction last at least ten, and of course you're always stuck behind them.

"Welcome to Subway, how can I help you?" a visor-clad employee asked.

"Hello, I'd like a sandwich," the businessman in front of me declared.

"Sure, Monsieur. What kind? We have all these

varieties," the employee said, indicating a menu board the customer clearly hadn't bothered to notice.

His eyes widened at the possibilities. "Um, how about Le Tuna." His shoulders visibly relaxed as he thought he had completed the only task required of him.

"OK, sir. And on what type of bread?"

"A baguette, please."

"I'm sorry but we don't have baguettes." The employee listed the five bread options.

"What would you recommend?" As someone who's worked in the food industry, I've never understood this question. Unless you're making the sandwich for me, I don't see what good it does to find out my preference.

"They're all delicious, sir. But with Le Tuna I'd recommend wheat bread."

"Great, great. I'll take that," he said with relief.

The employee then progressed through the next barrage of questions—cheese? bacon? toasted? Sweat formed on the customer's brow as he said yes to each option.

A melted tuna and mayonnaise mess popped out of the oven and the perky employee continued.

"And what toppings would you like?"

At this point the customer wished he had never set foot in this newfangled American establishment. French driving tests asked fewer questions and clearly, based on the way the French drive, less importance is placed on them.

"What are my choices?"

"You can choose any of the fresh veggies you see here," she said, indicating the selection with a wave of her arm.

His eyes widened. "Oh la la. Um, OK. I'll have lettuce… carrots… corn… and chicken."

Hold the phone. You're offered a large assortment of toppings and that's what you pick? First, I'm not even sure why carrots and corn are available but you certainly shouldn't choose them, not when you have lovely options like onions and cucumbers at your disposal. However, I'd gladly choose carrots and corn over chicken. On a tuna sandwich. Chicken isn't a topping, dude!

At this point his sandwich must have cost $20 and been pushing 4,000 calories with all the extra cheese and bacon and chicken. The bread was toasted and the cheese was melted, but it had visibly cooled off by now. Cold chicken perched awkwardly on top of his vegetable garden. I didn't know how it could get any worse.

"Which sauce would you like with that, sir?"

"Sauce? Oh no. What are my choices?"

Oh brother, here we go again. She ran through the six sauces.

"Which one would you recommend?"

At this point, no sauce would play nicely with the sandwich. He'd piled so many ingredients on it that he already had too many flavor profiles going on for any sauce in the world to pull it together.

"Sir, if I may, I'd suggest mayonnaise," I piped up.

"Oh yes, that sounds perfect. Thank you."

Anything to speed this up.

"Would you like chips and a drink with that?"

Another roadblock. I turned to Marie. "We're never going to make it back to the office on time."

"Oh who cares. You've been gone for four months, what's a few extra minutes?"

Touché.

18

Plus Sizes

As WINTER WORE ON, Mika and I settled into a routine. Our lives centered around Leo and work and trying to catch whatever sleep we could. I'd have the occasional drink during Sunday lunch with the in-laws, but overall we were pretty boring.

"I told you this would happen," Anne Marie said over the phone one evening. I could hear lots of commotion in the background, of the shaking-a-martini variety as opposed to shaking-a-rattle.

"I don't know why I didn't believe you. I'm so tired all the time and Leo is always moving or making noise or spitting up. I couldn't handle that with a hangover."

"You don't have to drink enough to have a hangover," she said.

Then we both laughed.

"Never mind. Stupid suggestion. We both know how you are."

She was right. I wasn't a one-glass-of-wine or one-fruity-cocktail kind of gal. I cleared out the entire stash of booze and left a path of destruction in my wake. I'd stumble home, leave a trail of clothes leading up to my bed, and wake up with a nasty hangover that wouldn't subside until well past sunset the next day. There's no way I could face that if I had to take care of my energetic son.

"You have fun, Ammo. Drink a few for me."

"Already did, but I'd be happy to have a few more."

Nowadays, the trail of clothes lying around was my son's. Between his reflux and diaper blow-outs and drool, that kid went through more outfit changes than an Oscar master of ceremonies.

And he outgrew his clothes before my eyes. He was a hefty chunk of a boy, despite having been a preemie, and got little use out of each item of clothing. He'd spit up, throw up or otherwise mess up his outfit and by the time it came out of the wash, it wouldn't fit.

"I don't understand it, Mika. Your aunt just gave us this nine-month onesie and it's already too tight for Leo. He's only six months old!"

"I don't get it either. But have you noticed his American clothes fit better?"

We'd been spoiled with numerous gifts from both sides of the family, from preppy French cardigans to jerseys supporting our favorite U.S. sports teams (Go Cardinals!). The six-month American onesies did fit better than the French ones.

"I wonder why that is. Are French babies smaller?"

"Have you seen the other kids at the *crèche*? Leo is one of the youngest but he is practically twice their size."

I had to investigate. I retrieved his *carnet de santé* from our file cabinet. This handy (handwritten, of course) book held all his medical records since birth. Between his initial hospital stay and subsequent diagnoses of torticollis, asthma, milk allergy, and numerous ear and bronchial infections, the booklet was jam-packed.

In the back was a growth chart where the doctor noted Leo's height and weight after each visit. He was consistently in the 80th percentile, which seemed about right to me. His meaty thighs would make a nice dinner but he wasn't obese.

Just for kicks, I grabbed one of my American baby books and flipped to the growth chart. With help from an online metric converter, I graphed Leo's measurements. According to the U.S. chart he was in the 60th percentile.

"I guess American babies are fatter," I said to Mika. "We'll have to remember to always buy a size or two bigger in France."

I hoped it wouldn't give Leo a complex.

❧

That weekend I rounded up a stash of Leo's unworn clothes and ventured out to exchange them for larger sizes.

"Bonjour, Madame. How can I help you?"

"Bonjour. I'd like to exchange these clothes for the next size up."

"Sure. Why don't you start browsing while I calculate your total?"

I perused the shop but couldn't find any of the same outfits. Hopefully she would let me exchange them for different clothes. Then again, this was France we were talking about.

I gathered up a few items in the 12-month size.

"Madame? Your total is €82. Are you ready to check out?"

"I think so." I'd been keeping a mental tally as I went, but it was hard to calculate exactly since some of the items were on sale. Whatever. It would be close enough.

The cashier tapped away on her register. "Oooh, I'm sorry," she said, as if she'd announced they'd stopped making Kraft mac and cheese forever. "Your total is only €81.04."

"OK, that's fine." I didn't see what the big deal was. She could issue me 96 cents change or put it on a gift card or just keep it.

"No, you don't understand, Madame. I can't do an exchange for less than the total. You have to have at least €82 worth of purchases."

Now why the hell was that? That made no sense. Surely she could find a way?

But she had already moved on to help the next customer. I was on my own to find one more item to raise my total.

I scanned the store but obviously nothing cost 96 cents. They had hideous socks and outrageous items that clearly were in their rightful place on the clearance rack. I looked over at the pile of clothes sitting by the register. Maybe I could swap an item out? No, that would require her to re-key everything.

We could be here all day.

I spotted an accessory rack and selected a gray conductor's hat. For €10. Great. I had to pay €9.04 to make my exchange. At least my son would have the proper headgear if he needed to drive a train.

At the next boutique, I asked straight-up about their return policy. Let's not waste time if they're all going to be the same.

This one was the same.

But at least I knew in advance. I embarked on a reverse The Price is Right quest—get as close to the target price while going over.

I found a ton of stylish clothes in the 12-month size but even they seemed small. I figured I'd play it safe and go with 18 months.

I set my stash on the check-out counter.

"Madame, just to be sure, you're exchanging these 9-month clothes for 18-month ones?"

"Yes, and even those don't look very large. I guess my baby is big for his age."

"How old is he?"

"Six months."

"Then his current size would be nine months, and since you say he's big, you should probably do twelve months. And if you are buying for the future then 18 months is just right."

"Okaaaaaaay. But I have a question. How come his size is nine months if he's only six months old, chubby legs aside?"

"That's because when you see on the tag '6 months' it really means '3-6 months.' If you want '6-9 months' then you have to buy '9 months.'"

How was I supposed to know that? "Why don't they write '6-9 months' on the tag?"

She was stumped. "Good question."

As she processed my transaction I reflected on how stupid this system was. It was bad enough my baby was considered fat by French standards and was bursting out of his fashionable seams. But it didn't help that their sizes were out of whack. It was like an expiration date: "Must be worn before baby reaches this age."

And while she had said that 6 months is really 3-6 months, how were the larger sizes calculated? Was I to assume that 18 months was 12-18 months? Or did they have a 15-month size? That would mean that 18-months meant 15-18 months. Was I supposed to line up all their available sizes and base my calculations on that? What if they were out of stock of 15-month clothes, thus forcing me to calculate the size as 12-18 months when the real size was 15-18 months? Was it that hard to add an extra number and a dash to the label?

I'd already spent way too much time pondering this. From now on I would buy clothes five sizes bigger than I needed. He'd grow into them eventually, right?

19

Poison Gift

MY IN-LAWS ARE AN EXTREMELY GENEROUS BUNCH. Not only do they bury us in baby clothes but they give thoughtful gifts for birthdays, Christmas, New Year's, Easter—you name it. My American family is a lovely bunch as well, but as I have fifty cousins, my aunts and uncles would go nuts trying to keep up with giving everyone gifts.

For some occasion or another, Mika's aunt gave us a Wonderbox called "Romantic Duo." Before your mind slips and falls in the gutter, let me explain.

Wonderbox is a brilliant concept that fails in execution because it's French. As the gift-giver, you select one of these pretty boxes based on the theme presented on the cover: Weekend Getaway, Relaxation and Well-Being, Gourmet Gurus, etc. Inside the box are a gift certificate and a thick booklet listing thousands of packages and places where you can allegedly use it.

The gift recipient opens said box and dreams of which package they'll choose. Dinner for two at a posh French restaurant? Couples massage and spa treatment? Photo shoot? The possibilities are endless!

Except you can't actually redeem the damn thing at any of the places listed in the book. You call the restaurant only to find out they're booked up for the next three years (yeah, right). You try for the spa treatment but they say the deal is no longer valid and you can only book manicures. A couples manicure? Thanks but no thanks.

"Bonjour, I'd like to book a photo shoot for me, my wife, and my son," Mika said politely down the phone line. "We have a Wonderbox gift certificate." As Leo was now a smiling six-month-old who could sit up on his own, we thought a family photo was the perfect use of our gift.

"Pardon me? You're in the booklet by mistake? How can that be?"

Yeah, how could that be? You mean the store accidentally provided Wonderbox with a photo of their studio, a package deal, a unique redemption code, and contact information? How do you do something like that on accident? Excuse me, *by* accident.

"I hear you, ma'am, but I don't see how that's our fault. Can we please still use the gift certificate? The package we'd like to book is €150 over the value of the gift certificate so we'd still be paying that portion."

How could they argue with that? We'd be dropping a hefty sum for a few snaps of a camera lens, so gift certificate aside, they were still getting a good deal.

"Yes, I did see that the gift certificate was only valid for a photo with two people. Could we pay extra to include our baby in the photo?"

I don't know why we should have to pay extra for Leo when it wouldn't cost them any extra but Mika was being totally reasonable. We were basically signing our paycheck over to this chick. Surely she would say yes?

But no, Mika hung up the phone without saying another word.

"What happened?" I asked.

"She said, 'No, I'm sorry, I can't help you' and hung up!"

"What the heck? She didn't even attempt to book an appointment without using the gift certificate?"

"No, and she didn't even say goodbye!"

Clearly this part of her impoliteness was what really got my French husband's goat.

"Unbelievable. We were ready to throw several hundred euros at them and they just hung up on us? Idiots."

∽∾

"I have a surprise for you," Mika said one Saturday morning. "Leo and I are going to have 'Guy's Day Out' at the playground while you get a spa treatment. You need to be ready by 1:00. Sound good?"

Um, yes!

"What's the occasion?" I asked.

"No occasion, other than I love my wife. Plus I used the Wonderbox."

"No way! That's even better than loving your wife! But wait, I thought we had to do a couples massage?"

"You know I'm too ticklish for a massage. I found a place that let me use the value of the gift certificate on a package all for you. It involves full body exfoliation and a massage."

"Have I ever told you you're the best?"

∽∾

That afternoon I arrived for my appointment ready to unwind. I loved Leo to pieces but was looking forward to some alone time.

Stucco walls enclosed the Moroccan-themed spa, where

a colorful mosaic floor stretched wall-to-wall and a marble fountain gurgled in the corner.

"Bonjour, my name is Leila. Would you like a mint tea while you wait?" The exotic-looking beautician handed me the tea cup with a smile.

The prudish American in me was worried this would be more like a *hammam* than the girly spas I'd been to in the U.S. At least my doctor's appointments had eliminated nearly all remaining modesty in my life.

When I finished my tea, Leila indicated for me to follow her to the massage room.

"Undress and lie on the bed and I'll return in a few minutes."

Easy enough. I undressed and looked around for the disposable undies spas usually offered.

They were nowhere to be found. OK, so, yeah, I was in a *hammam*. This lady was going to rub down my completely naked body.

Leila knocked on the door and then entered. Why even bother with doors in this place? We're all naked here! Just kidding, please don't take the doors off.

"Are you ready, Madame?"

What a silly question. I was lying face down, unclothed on the bed. If I'd meant to do anything else first, I probably should have done it before I was buck naked.

"Oui."

"And are you something-something?"

"Pardonnez-moi?"

"You're not something-something, are you?"

Huh? I couldn't bear to make her repeat it again, so using her tone as a cue I answered, "No."

"OK, I'll start."

She dipped her hand into a bucket of warm sludge and slathered it up and down my legs. I recognized the sweet nutty smell of argon oil. My stomach growled and I craved a peanut butter and jelly sandwich.

The scrub felt amazing, except those hands kept rubbing dangerously close to some personal bits. When she worked her way down to my feet, it tickled like crazy. I could hardly hold still.

"Madame, you're not something-something?"

OK, seriously, what the hell was something-something?

"No," I insisted, even though I still had no idea what she was talking about.

She finished my back, then flipped me over and did the front. If I wasn't so chilled out, I would have blushed at the treatment I was getting.

Then she wrapped me in plastic and cranked the dial on the space heater.

"Reposez-vous, Madame. I'll be back in twenty minutes."

Soothing Arabic instrumental music played in the background as I baked in my plastic covering. I briefly wondered how I was going to wash this gunk off, but relaxation overtook me and I drifted off to sleep.

"Madame, please come with me."

Wow, that was a quick twenty minutes. Leila stood in the doorway, light from the bright hallway shining into my dim tranquil chamber.

"You can shower off across the hall."

Across the hall? Was she kidding me?

Her no-nonsense expression indicated she was not.

I scooted off the bed, then waddled my naked, nutty-sludge-plastic-wrapped booty across the hall with as much dignity as I could muster. She peeled off the wrap, leaving my naked, nutty-sludge covered body in the middle of the shower. The fluorescent lights of the room hid nothing.

She turned on the water then left me to it.

I hosed off in the warm shower, steam filling the stall as I splashed argon goop all over the walls. Once free of the muddy mixture, I turned off the shower and scanned the room for a towel.

No towel. Crap! Why hadn't I checked before I'd hopped in the shower? Oh please don't tell me I have to walk back across the hall without even my plastic wrap to protect me!

Leila returned in the nick of time and handed me a plush towel. Well hello, there, Leila. Meet my naked body! Oh wait, you two have already met.

"Come with me, Madame, and we will finish your treatment."

৩৯২

After an hour of soothing massage and another mint tea for the road, I was on my way. Mika and Leo met me outside, both with chocolate on the corners of their mouths.

"How was it?"

"Wonderful. Once I got past the whole being naked thing. But man, I'm more ticklish than I realized."

"You see? That's why I don't get massages. I don't like *chatouilles*."

"*Chat*-what?"

"*Chatouilles*. You know, tickles."

Ah, it made sense now. When Leila had asked if I was "something-something" she'd been asking if I was ticklish. And like a stubborn fool I'd insisted I wasn't, even while giggling and squirming.

Was I ever going to learn French?

20

Spring and Water Are in the Air

SPRING ROLLED AROUND and we ventured out to explore our neighborhood. Our apartment was close to the Promenade Plantée, a three-mile elevated walking path with a wide variety of trees, shrubbery, and flowers.

The French are ingenious like that—they take an unused railway structure and convert it into something that is both functional and beautiful.

Of course, getting on that thing with a stroller is a bitch.

Parts of it are several stories high, so you are faced with numerous flights of stairs or a broken elevator. Seriously, I've never seen any of the elevators working.

But the flowery viaduct is so darned pretty that Mika and I would heft the stroller up what felt like two hundred steps in order to have our relaxing walk.

Wooden benches, with the green paint peeling at the edges, line the path. They're often populated with homeless people enjoying a warm can of beer or teenagers smoking cigarettes away from their parents' eyes. You'll occasionally hear a rustling in the bushes, but it's rarely a wild animal, unless you count amorous adolescents and urinating homeless men as wild.

Signs dot the trail, identifying the different species of wildlife that live in the area. I may not know how to say "tickle" in French but I know two different words for "bat"—*pipistrelle*, which is the cutest word ever, and *chauvre souris*, literally "bald mouse."

Pub quiz, here I come!

About halfway down the Promenade, the path reaches ground level (or, more accurately, the ground rises to meet the path level) so you can get off the trail without having to wrestle with more stairs. We usually exited at that point and took a roundabout way back home, passing a street of lovely Georgian-style homes that felt more like London than Paris.

"I wonder why there's just that one row of houses built in that style?" I asked Mika.

"I've always wondered that myself. It's funny because I normally like the Parisian Haussmanian style, yet this street is one of my favorites."

"Same here! It seems so—"

But before we could delve further into our amateur architecture discussion, a huge downpour of water fell right on Leo's head.

"What the hell?" we both shouted, running around the sides of the stroller. Leo instantly erupted into tears, as you do when a huge blast of water falls from the sky.

Mika removed his hoodie to dry Leo off with while I searched in the diaper bag for a burp cloth.

"Hey, what kind of *connard* throws water out a window?" a tall, lanky teen shouted up at the building we stood in front of. His two friends joined in.

"That's what happened?" I asked, addressing the kids.

"Yeah, we saw it. Some old guy dumped a bucket of

water out the window. I know him, too. I live in this building. Don't worry, Madame, I'll go talk to him and let him know he hurt a kid. He won't be doing it again."

That hadn't even occurred to me. Was this guy a serial bucket dumper? The chances of us walking under his window at the exact moment he had dumped the bucket were slim, so I doubted it could ever happen again. However, I've been struck by lightning and that's not likely to happen either.

"Thanks, that's nice of you," I said. "Bonne journée."

I turned back to my husband and son. Leo had already gotten over it, sucking contentedly on his pacifier.

I shuddered to think what had been in that water. Dirty mop water? The contents of an old fishbowl? Something worse that I couldn't even imagine?

"I can't believe someone would so carelessly splash water out a window. And then to have it end up on my baby!" Mika shouted.

If I was Mama Bear, Mika was the meanest Papa Bear around. Normally a chill guy, Mika bared his teeth at any threat to his child.

"I know. That guy is a mega douche."

We strolled in silence, Mika likely plotting some Godfather-style revenge on the old man while my thoughts were elsewhere. Specifically, on Baby #2.

"So, I know Leo's not even one year old yet, but maybe we should start thinking about Baby #2 sometime soon?" I ventured. "We said we wanted our kids close in age."

"Yeah, totally. We're already sleep-deprived and losing our minds, so why not have another one?"

It sounded facetious but he was serious. And it made total sense. If you wait until the first child is more independent and grown-up, then it will be a bigger shock to go back to sleepless nights and diaper blow-outs.

Our social lives were pretty much non-existent at that point, so as long as we were already staying home every night, fawning over our son and not drinking alcohol, why not throw another noisemaker into the mix?

"We'll need a bigger apartment, though," I said. "We're already crammed into that tiny bedroom as it is. There is literally no place to put another baby."

"There's always the closet," Mika said with a chuckle. "But yeah, you're right. We'll need a bigger apartment before we have another baby. So... maybe let's wait until the end of the summer? I don't have it in me to do another apartment search just yet."

"I don't think I have it in me to watch another guy stick his hand on a burner. So it's decided. End of the summer."

ॐৣৣ৶

"Can you make it to my going-away party?" Marie asked. "I know it's hard with Leo but it's going to be at the Long Hop."

Going-away parties are at the top of the list of Events You Can't Miss, right next to weddings, birthday parties, and George Michael concerts. Throw in alcohol and schedule it at my favorite bar, and you've made me an offer I can't refuse.

"Of course I can come! Work isn't going to be the same without you. So let's get drunk and forget about it!"

Marie had quit her job to move to the French countryside and write a book. I would have been jealous if I wasn't so darn happy for her. Plus, as an author, she could provide quality feedback on my book (which she did, and you can thank her for how awesome it is).

That Friday night I was ready for Mama's First Big Night Out Since Leo Was Born. He was eight months old. As a former party girl and bathroom-floor-sleeper, this night was long overdue.

True to form, I drank too much, sang too loudly, and

had way too much fun. I had completely forgotten about the time, and when I checked my phone, noting three missed calls from Mika, I was shocked to see it was already 1:00 am. The last time I'd been up at that hour was to clean up baby vomit.

And if I didn't call it a night soon, I'd risk cleaning up my own vomit.

"Marie, I hate to do this but I have to go home. I need to catch the last Métro."

"No problem! I'll go with you."

We stumbled out of the bar and headed up the street to Notre Dame. We sang (shouted) every song from "The Little Mermaid" as we made our way to the Marais, where Marie lived and where I would catch Line 1 home.

"The seaweed is always greener, in somebody else's lake!"

"Le roseau est toujours plus vert, dans le marais d'à côté!"

We continued our melodious tune, me singing in English, Marie singing in French, arms hanging around each other's shoulders, until we came face-to-face with two guys, similarly drunk, with their arms around each other's shoulders.

"You girls are American? We love Americans," they slurred.

I was about to correct them and point out that Marie had been singing in French so their assumption was stupid (because I'm nice like that), but Marie said, "Yes, I am American. U.S.A.! U.S.A.!"

We played along, pretending Marie was from New York and these idiots bought it. Marie's English is perfect but she still has an accent.

"Would you American ladies like to see what a real Frenchman is like?"

And… we're done. Gag me.

"Sure! Let me just call my husband and check on my

baby," I said.

They looked confused for a second until they realized that was my way of blowing them off.

"You're missing out!" they shouted, as they continued down the street, searching for girls who would actually go home with them.

"You're so mean, Vicki!" Marie said.

"Hey, I have a Métro to catch. I don't have time to waste with those fools."

"I'm gonna miss your sass."

"I'll miss you too."

The next day I didn't have time to miss much of anything or anyone. I woke up with a nasty hangover. At 5:00 am. To the sound of Leo crying and smacking the rail of his crib.

Ughhhhh.

This house was too small and my headache was way too big for this.

"Hey, Mika? The time has come to switch sides in our bed. You're on Leo duty from now on. See you in a few hours. And I'll like you ten times more if there's greasy food waiting for me when I wake up."

When I dragged myself out of bed at 9:00 am, Mika had two Egg McMuffins waiting for me.

"Ready to have another baby, Mommy?"

"Coffee, please."

He poured me a cup. "Some night, eh?"

"You know, honestly, I *am* ready for another baby. Last night was awesome but this morning suuuuuuuuuuuuuucks. I think I got it all out of my system."

"OK, drunko."

"I swear! I'm too old for this crap. This summer, let's do this thing."

Confessions Before Baby #2

I UNDERSTOOD WHY MIKA WANTED TO WAIT until the end of the summer before even thinking about Baby #2. We could enjoy a few more months of carefree life (well, as much as you can when you already have an infant) and we could postpone looking for an apartment just a bit longer.

It would be way easier to house-hunt after the dead of summer, when Parisians close up shop and all that's left in the usually-bustling capital are tourists and a few scraps of trash blowing in the wind.

Plus Leo would be one year old by then and he would magically become an easy baby. His pediatrician had told us he could outgrow his milk allergy by then and even his asthma might be less severe, particularly since we faithfully endured his twice-daily nebulization sessions/screaming matches.

Two babies can't be that much harder than one. I don't know what people are complaining about. And two babies close together actually seems easier. You already have all the gear and you're already in the zombie, sleep-deprived mindset.

I was pretty much done with drinking and ready to try for Baby #2. If I wasn't going to be dancing on bars, might as well get this show on the road. I really didn't want to have to wait until the end of summer.

But I wasn't going to be sneaky about it. I promised Mika we would wait until we had moved to yet another new address.

21

Here We Go Again

DURING PREVIOUS APARTMENT SEARCHES, Mika and I had been relatively easygoing. Bathroom inside the apartment? Check. Electricity that worked at least half the time? Sounds good. No elevator? No problem! Saves money on a gym membership.

But with a one-year-old and everything that entails—strollers, baby bathtubs, high chairs, massive quantities of clothes and burp cloths and bibs—we needed more space. Particularly since we were hoping to welcome another addition to our family.

Our updated list of requirements included:

1. No higher than the French first floor (meaning, up one flight of stairs).

2. Place to park our stroller (preferably out of view of an overly helpful concierge).

3. Two bedrooms (the kids could share—we were dreaming if we thought we could get a three-bedroom

place in Paris without winning the lottery or selling our souls or both).

4. A bathroom where I could use the toilet without my knees touching the door.

5. No more than a twenty-minute walk to Leo's *crèche* (we had been fortunate to get accepted to this one; we'd never luck out again anywhere else).

6. At least 50 square meters (540 square feet) and no more than €1,300 per month ($1,800).

Americans reading this are saying, "That's it? I'd be asking for way more square footage and a lower price, not to mention another bedroom and a few extras like a balcony, washer/dryer hook-ups, and a parking spot."

Parisians reading this are snorting, "Good luck finding a hole in the ground for that price."

Our new standards were high and we knew we'd have trouble finding a place. But what was the point of moving (again) if it wasn't going to be better than the place we had? I'd cram that second baby in the closet before I'd move to yet another cramped, overpriced apartment.

Mika took his time checking out rental listings. Three years younger than me, his biological clock wasn't ticking quite as quickly for Baby #2. Plus, as we promised, we were waiting until the end of the summer for that. No rush.

Each apartment we visited had something wrong with it. The listing would say the apartment was on the ground floor (yay, no stairs!) but then there would be a flight of stairs to enter the building (so, in fact, there *were* stairs). Or Google Maps would promise it was a twenty-minute walk to the *crèche*, but in case your robotic legs were broken that day, it was more like a forty-minute walk.

We visited a three-bedroom apartment that was slightly out of our price range and needed several coats of paint, but giddy with the idea of all that space, we submitted our dossier anyway. Rejected.

We were about to give up when Catherine saved the day. "Would you consider a *2-3 pièce?*" she asked over coffee and croissants one Sunday morning.

French apartment listings count the number of *pièces*, or rooms, as opposed to bedrooms. Therefore a *3-pièce* is likely an apartment with a living room and two bedrooms, but is technically just a three-room apartment. You could find a living room, dining room, and bedroom. Or three bedrooms and no living room. Or a living room, bedroom, and torture chamber.

You were totally taking a chance.

With a *2-3 pièce* I didn't even know what that meant. Don't you know if you have two or three rooms?

"What the heck is that?" I asked, my mouth full of my favorite pastry.

"It means there's one normal-sized room and then one large room that is likely somehow divided. It can probably easily be converted into a *3-pièce*. Maybe you would get your two bedrooms that way, but since it's a little unconventional it would be cheaper."

Which made sense—it sounded like such an apartment would be made of Legos, so it should be less expensive.

"Good idea, Mom," Mika said. "I'll broaden my search criteria to include that.

It was worth a shot.

∽⌇⌇

"I found it!" Mika said. "This is the one! This apartment meets all of our criteria. We have an appointment to view it tonight. And for once, we'll be the only people at the visit."

This sounded too good to be true.

"Great! But let's not get our hopes up."

The minute we saw the place, we couldn't help but get our hopes up. It was perfect. The building was immaculate and even had a parking garage for strollers. The apartment was on the second floor (OK, one floor higher than we'd wanted) but the building had an elevator. And the apartment was situated directly over a large arched walkway leading to a square courtyard with a park in the center of it, which meant that there was no apartment beneath it. Which meant the pitter patter of little feet wouldn't annoy any neighbors below.

The layout was logical (which can't always be said of French apartments, which are often converted into maze-like dwellings) and the apartment didn't need any work done. I checked the bathroom and was able to close the door with room to spare. Did you hear me? ROOM TO SPARE.

The *2-3 pièces* thing wasn't even that weird. It was a big living room with a floor-to-ceiling wall cutting halfway across the middle of it. With careful furniture arrangement we could convert the back half of the room into our bedroom, keep the living room as-is, and put the kids in the bedroom. Not glamorous by American standards but this was livin' large in Paris.

And, as if in a dream, it even had a walk-in closet. A closet! That you could walk into! We could stash our clothes there, meaning we wouldn't need a dresser in our living-bedroom. Or we could use the closet as a nursery. Just kidding. Kind of.

"We'll take it!" we shouted in unison.

"Great," the agent said, paging through our dossier. "I'll run the numbers tomorrow morning and will get back to you as soon as it's confirmed."

We tried not to get too excited. We'd been rejected from worse apartments before, and this one was a chateau compared to them. No way could we be this lucky.

☙❧

"Guess what?" Mika asked over the phone the next day.

"What?" I asked, taking a bite of my baguette sandwich. I was on my lunch break at work, sitting on a park bench, enjoying the last days of summer sun.

"We got the apartment."

"No way!" I'd tried not to think about it for the past 18 hours, fearful I'd only be disappointed. But we were now the proud renters of a 53 square meter 2-3 room apartment, all for the low price of €1,350 per month. "When do we move in?"

"We sign the lease tonight and we can move in a month."

"I'd say this is a champagne-worthy occasion!"

Might as well squeeze in a few more drinks before getting pregnant.

22

Being John Malkovich

EVERY TIME I BRUISED MY KNEE on our bathroom door, I was so glad we'd be moving to a larger (but still small, mind you) apartment.

"All set for the move!" Mika said, hanging up the phone. He'd booked a moving van and his uncle and cousin volunteered to help. "Philippe and Florian will arrive in the early afternoon and my mom and dad will babysit Leo."

On Saturday, I opened the door to greet my in-laws, giving the routine four cheek-kisses.

"This doesn't look too bad," Uncle Philippe said, seeing I'd already packed everything into boxes and lined them up neatly by the front door.

"We can get this done in no time," said Florian, with the confidence of a twenty-one-year-old guy.

I let the men move the heavy furniture while I made trip after trip up and down the stairs and across the courtyard with the boxes. Funny how it can look like it's not that much stuff until you have to spend two hours schlepping it. And this was after I'd donated five bags of stuff to charity and sold a slew of items on Craigslist.

We finally slammed the door to the overloaded van and hopped in the front for the two-minute drive to our new address.

"Unloading will be easier. You have an elevator, right?" Philippe asked.

"Yep. We've never used it since we're on the second floor, but it should help."

It didn't.

Grab yourself a cup of coffee and get comfortable, because it's going to take me a while to explain just how stupid this elevator was.

For starters, it was accessible via the half-floor, not the ground floor. The seven-story stairwell was split so that you had the "0th floor" (ground floor), then eight steps to the "1/2th floor" landing where you could access the elevator. Then eight more steps to the 1st floor and so on. At a minimum, you'd have to get everything up eight steps.

"Let's do this thing!" Florian announced with gusto.

He, Philippe, and Mika heaved our bed frame up the steps and pressed the button for the elevator. It dinged and Mika pulled open the door (because on top of its other flaws, the elevator didn't have automatic doors either).

Philippe peeked his head in. "This is it? It's less than a square meter! I'm not sure two people could even fit in there."

I peered around him and saw what he meant. Wow. That was one tiny elevator.

"Bummer. Do you guys mind taking the bed up the stairs? I can use the elevator for the boxes."

While they lugged the bed frame up one and a half more flights, I started carrying boxes up to the 1/2th floor. Once I had a full load, I packed everything in the elevator.

Mika had finished with the bed and met me on the

1/2th floor landing.

"How about you take the elevator," I suggested, "and I'll meet you up there to help unload." I figured he could use a break after moving the bed, even just a short elevator ride.

I walked up the remaining flights to wait for the elevator. Something was wrong, but I couldn't immediately figure it out. I blame it on baby brain, even though my son was one year old.

"Vicki?"

"Mika?"

It sounded like his voice was coming from above.

"Where are you?" he asked.

"Where are *you*?"

"There was no button for the second floor so I'm on the third floor."

Bingo. I'd figured out the problem. I was on the second floor and was staring at a translucent piece of glass where an elevator door should have been. I was confused because it kind of looked like the elevator should have been able to stop there but now I noticed there were no buttons and no doors. See? Baby brain.

I paused to consider the best course of action. It was six of one, half dozen of the other. If Mika rode the elevator down, he would stop at the 1/2th floor and we'd have to carry everything up one and a half flights to the apartment. As he was on the third floor (well, 3 1/2th floor) we would have to carry everything down one and a half flights.

"This is insane! I'm coming up," I shouted as I mounted the stairs. At least carrying the loads down would be slightly easier than going up.

But seriously, what was up with that elevator? Why did it stop on the half-floor landing? And then not stop at all on the second floor? I blamed myself for not checking it out before signing the lease but I didn't think that verifying the elevator actually stopped at my floor was something I needed to check.

Even if it did stop on my floor, technically I'd still have to walk up a half-flight to get on the elevator, then walk down a half flight from the 2 1/2th floor to get to my apartment. What was the point of taking an elevator for two floors if you still had to take one flight of stairs? And since it didn't even stop on the 2 1/2th floor, I'd have to get out at the 3 1/2th floor, and descend one and a half flights, totaling two full flights. That's the same as just walking the whole way up and not even messing with the elevator!

I vowed then and there to never use the elevator again. I couldn't imagine a single scenario where it would actually save me any time or trouble.

"Thanks for the help," I said, cracking open beers for the guys once the last of the furniture had been hauled inside.

"Too bad the elevator was a bust," Philippe said.

While they finished their beers, I surveyed the work to be done. The neat-freak in me wanted to unpack and set up the apartment right away. But the rational person in me knew I didn't have much time. I'd free the guys to go chill at Mika's parents' house while I at least got the beds ready for the night. I could just ignore the rest of the chaos.

Yeah right.

"I'll meet you over there in a bit and then Mika and I will order pizza for everyone. Thanks again," I said, practically shoving them out the door. If I hurried, I could not only set up the beds but I could at least somewhat organize the boxes so that my just-starting-to-walk little troublemaker wouldn't be able to cause quite as much trouble.

After an hour, I had to call it quits or else I'd risk being rude to my in-laws. Catherine and Gilbert had been babysitting all afternoon and I was sure everyone was hungry by that point.

As I grabbed my keys, I heard odd sounds coming from the hallway, like banging on a piano. Was someone playing a piano in the hallway? Or was their front door open? Were these walls paper thin? If so, the neighbors were about to learn just how loud a one-year-old could be.

I opened my front door and ran into a greasy moving guy. A piano was wedged between the stairs and the landing. Two equally slimy moving guys were on the other side of the piano, down a few steps.

That explained the sounds I'd heard. But I didn't understand how these guys had gotten stuck. They made it up all the other flights of stairs and were only now encountering issues? Just do what you did for each previous flight, dummies!

Of course, they couldn't make any progress now that I was on the scene. They were too distracted by my sloppy ponytail and delicious musky odor after a long day of moving.

Did they have no standards?

The guy on the landing sidled up to me, standing so close that his leg literally touched my leg. "My, don't you look pretty tonight." He licked his lips.

Ew, ew, ew. I fumbled with my keys, trying to lock up, but the medieval contraption looked more suited to locking wrongdoers in dungeons. I couldn't get the darn thing to turn in the keyhole.

"You and I could have a gooooood time tonight, oh yeah." His breath reeked of alcohol. I could practically see fumes escaping his mouth as he chatted me up.

I finally got the key to work, then turned around, my face bumping into his moustache. Gross.

"You wanna party tonight?" he asked, rubbing his thigh up my sweaty jeans.

How was I going to get out of this?

The piano was blocking the stairwell but I sure as heck wasn't going to stay there and let that perv hump my leg. It would probably take me twenty minutes to unlock my door, and besides, I couldn't stay trapped in my apartment all night. My family was waiting for me!

"Sure! Let's totally party. First, I need to go to my mother-in-law's house for dinner. And I'll need to put my son to bed. But maybe my husband and I can meet you here in a few hours?"

His face fell as he realized I was making fun of him. "You don't have to be so nasty about it, bitch."

Oh yes, I'm the nasty one in this situation.

I squeezed past him and did the only thing I could—I walked up to the 3 1/2th floor to ride the elevator down. I pressed the button and waited impatiently, checking behind me every few seconds for signs of the creepy dude.

Once the elevator arrived, I thrust open the door, hopped in, and scanned the buttons for "0." It was then that I noticed the elevator's final quirk. Not only did it not stop on the second floor, it didn't stop on *any* even-numbered floors. Which seems to be more consistent, until you think about it (which of course I did).

In total, the elevator stopped at 0, 3, 5, and 7, or technically 0.5, 3.5, 5.5, and 7.5. Zero is even and one is odd, so it wasn't even consistent between odds and evens.

Maybe the builders thought people on lower floors didn't need an elevator? But that didn't explain why it didn't stop at the fourth or sixth floor (or 4.5 and 6.5).

Why go through the trouble of installing an elevator if it's only going to stop at four out of the eight floors? Is it really that much harder to put doors on each level?

And one last question—who the hell manufactures (and is subsequently able to sell) an elevator that only has buttons for four out of the eight floors?

I can imagine the conversation between the rocket scientist who devised this plan and the knucklehead who went along with it:

"Hi, I'd like to install an elevator in my building but I

don't need it to stop at all floors. I'm thinking maybe half of them will be good enough. Say, all the odd-numbered floors? You got any pre-made elevators with buttons to match my ridiculous request?"

"You're in luck, pal. We've got one with buttons for 0, 3, 5, and 7. Will that work?"

"Close enough! While we're at it, I want the absolutely-no-frills option. None of them fancy automatic doors."

"Wouldn't dream of it."

"And the elevator itself should be smaller than a phone booth. I don't want any parties in there."

"We're totally on the same page, sir."

"Excellent. You've got yourself a deal. Oh wait, one more thing. I'm toying with the idea of stopping on the half-floor instead of the actual floor."

"Like in the movie *Being John Malkovich*? That 7 1/2th floor was hilarious."

"I know! You so get me. But should we... oh never mind. I was going to ask if we should put the '1/2' on the button but that would be confusing. Let's just keep it simple."

At that moment, despite being the world's most useless elevator, I couldn't have loved it more. It had saved the day, whisking me away from the leg-humping delivery guy.

23

Positively Nauseated

ONCE WE WERE SETTLED in our new apartment, I didn't waste a second before nagging Mika about Baby #2.

"Babe," Mika said. "I promised once we moved. We moved. I want this as much as you do."

Cool. I whipped out my calendar and prepared to do some calculations. In case you haven't noticed by now, I'm a math nerd and I'm not very chill. On rare occasions I'm caught unprepared (hello, early arrival of Baby #1) but most things in my life are the result of meticulous planning. I couldn't survive in a bureaucratic country like France all these years if I didn't have my act together.

I ran my finger across the days of September, then flipped back to August. Hold on a minute. Something was up. I didn't want to alarm Mika so I kept my mouth shut.

That was really hard to do.

Luckily, I'd stocked up on pregnancy tests (See? Prepared.) but as you're really supposed to do it first thing in the morning, I'd have to wait until the next day.

"Good night, honey," I said, kissing Mika as I settled into bed.

"G'night," he mumbled, already half asleep even though his head had only hit the pillow seconds earlier. We were perpetually tired chasing after our energetic one-year-old.

At four in the morning I woke up and needed to go to the bathroom. I knew what that likely meant, but did the pregnancy test anyway.

Even without my contact lenses in, I could see that bright blue plus sign before I had finished going to the bathroom. Side note: that's something TV shows always get wrong. Labor and delivery take about as long as it takes for the results of a pregnancy test to show up; that is, five minutes. Do any TV shows have mothers on their writing staff?

I climbed back into bed, wanting to share the news with Mika but not wanting to wake him. His grizzly bear snores told me he was fast asleep. The news could wait until the morning. I didn't know if I could, though.

The alarm went off and I rushed to get to the bathroom first. As I had a stash of pregnancy tests, it couldn't hurt to use another one.

Same result. Positive.

"Morning, sunshine," Mika said as we crossed in the hallway. He kissed me on the cheek. "Sleep well?"

"Yeah, you?"

"Like a rock."

I know. "So, um, guess what? Looks like I'm pregnant." I showed him the pregnancy test I'd been hiding off to my side. I probably shouldn't have sprung it on him before his morning cup of coffee but I'd already had to contain the secret for an unbearable three hours.

"Wow. Cool. Great. Wow. Um, but how?"

I'd been asking myself the same question. We both knew where babies came from but I hadn't seen any storks recently. We'd planned to wait until September before even trying so I couldn't quite believe I was already a month along.

"It must be an Immaculate Conception," I suggested. There was no other explanation. Between taking care of Leo and trying to sleep in an apartment without air-conditioning during another hot summer, I couldn't believe any procreation had happened. Then again, I was so sleep-deprived I couldn't be sure of much these days.

"Well, I guess that's one less thing to worry about," I said. "Job done!"

"Yeah, cool," Mika said, though not sounding entirely convinced.

৩৵৶

It took about a week for it to sink in for Mika. It's not that he wasn't happy about it—we were both thrilled—it's just that we had thought we'd have a little more time.

"Oh well, one month doesn't really change anything," Mika said once reality hit. "So let's see… that would make her due date May 20th?"

"According to the French way of counting, yes. The American due date is May 13th."

We both wrinkled our noses. 5/13/14. Odd numbers all over the place. "Maybe he or she will be born on April 30th, so we get an even birthday," I suggested. "Ooooh, or maybe April 24th, my half-birthday! Wouldn't that be cool? Just like Leo's birthday is your half-birthday!"

"Yeah, but we don't want to wish for our baby to be born early. I'll take an odd-numbered birthday if it means the baby's healthy and not a preemie."

"True. I guess we'll see."

৩৵৶

While it'd taken Mika a while for reality to hit, it had hit me just minutes after the plus sign appeared on the pregnancy test. I'd been lucky not to have morning sickness with Leo but I was nauseated 24/7 with Baby #2. And I was even more tired since I'd already been taking care of a toddler.

"It's weird," I said, trying to get ready for work while Leo pulled everything out of our bathroom cabinet. "As soon as I found out I was pregnant, I started feeling queasy and tired."

"Yeah, weird."

I could tell Mika didn't really believe me but he was too nice to say anything. Maybe it *was* psychological but I sure felt sick.

"You know what I just realized? I was pregnant when we were moving, hefting all those boxes up the stairs." Hrm, I hadn't felt tired during all of that physical exertion. Maybe it was all in my head.

My morning commute was pretty rough. Sometimes I lucked out and found a seat on the Métro but usually I didn't. The trains aren't air-conditioned so when you cram hundreds of people in during the still-warm September air, it quickly becomes stifling.

Add nausea to the mix and each ride was hell on wheels. Plus, even though pregnant women have the right to a seat, at one month along I was nowhere near showing yet (not that I was thin, mind you, but I didn't yet have a prominent baby bump).

I usually suffered in silence, counting down the stations until my stop.

One day, however, I just couldn't handle it. I had broken into a cold sweat, despite having stripped down to a sleeveless shirt and dress pants. I had no more articles of clothing to remove unless I wanted to be one of *those* people on the Métro.

Suits crowded around me, clueless to my plight. At

times like this, you're really not supposed to sit on the seats that flip down because it takes up twice the room in an already-packed space. But after a few stops, the crowd thinned slightly and I seized my chance. I thrust the seat down and fell into it. I looked like a jerk for sitting while everyone else was scrambling for a spot, but it was better than fainting and making the whole Métro stop, thus backing up the entire line.

I implemented the international sign for "I don't feel well" by placing my elbow on my knee and my forehead in my palm while keeping my head down. Anyone with half a brain cell would notice the glistening of my green-hued skin and be able to tell I wasn't feeling my best.

But the douchebag standing next to me clearly had no brain cells. He passive-aggressively[8] bumped my head with his laptop bag, muttering under his breath "C'est pas possible."

Most people in my place would ignore this guy and go about their miserable business. Instead, I straddled both ends of the tolerance spectrum. On the one hand, I felt guilty about sitting when the Métro was crowded. If someone didn't see that I was sick, they would think I was a jerk and I don't like to disappoint people like that.

On the other hand, I was sick and pregnant and had every right to be seated. No one forced these people to hop on a crowded train. They could have waited for the next one. And for sure, I didn't deserve to be on the receiving end of this guy's battering ram.

---

[8] I'm not sure I understand the term "passive-aggressive." Doesn't it seem like the guy's move is simply aggressive? He's purposely beating up a chick with his laptop just because she's sitting down. What part of that is passive? I guess it's the fact that he's acting like his bag is doing the pushing instead of him. So if he were to slap me, that's when we call it plain old "aggressive"? Seems like "passive-aggressive" lets people off the hook too easily. How about we call it "douchebag-aggressive"?

Some people may think, "It was her choice to get pregnant. Why should I have to give up my seat/suffer/be a decent human being?" And those people may think they have a good point, little smartasses. It's their right to never have children of their own. But back in the day, their mother was pregnant with them. Would they say that to their mom? Would they make their pregnant mother stand while they sat? Would they applaud anyone else who did?

Didn't think so.

I needed to unleash my wrath. I'd been nice long enough.

I waited for the next jolt to my head, followed by him mumbling, "This girl really needs to stand up."

I rose slowly, hoping I didn't get dizzy and faint.

"Finally!" he exclaimed, beaming at the other passengers as if he had cured cancer and deserved a round of applause.

"Excusez-moi, Monsieur. I'm pregnant and I'm not feeling well. That's why I was sitting."

"Oh, pardonnez-moi!" he exclaimed. "Please, then, sit down," he said, gesturing to the seat I'd just abandoned.

"No, no, Monsieur. You wanted me to stand. You repeated it multiple times and reinforced the point by beating my head with your bag. I will stand, since that's what you wanted."

A few snickers erupted around me.

"No, no, Madame, I apologize. Please sit down."

"Oh no, Monsieur. I wouldn't want to be rude. I had thought it was obvious when I was sitting with my head in my hands that I wasn't feeling well. But since it's not obvious, I wouldn't want anyone else on this train to be offended by a pregnant lady sitting down. I will stand."

"You could have said you were pregnant."

"So instead of focusing on not fainting I should communicate my current status to every passenger on the train? Or maybe you wanted me to make a sign? Is that it?

First you want me to stand, now you want me to make a sign. Is there anything else you would like me to do, Monsieur?" I was shouting at this point and everyone's attention was on us.

"No, Madame, I do not want you to make a sign. I'm sorry, I didn't know you were pregnant."

"But rather than give me the benefit of the doubt[9], you hit me in the head. Numerous times. Do you think I'm an asshole? Sitting on the Métro when it's crowded?"

I had a full-on audience now, and they were all laughing.

"No, Madame, I do not think you're an asshole. Please, I beg of you. Sit down."

"So noooooooooow, I get a seat. Why thank you, Monsieur. It's so nice of you to offer me my own seat back. But I'm fine, I will stand."

His face was bright red. Several people shouted "jerk" or "asshole" or worse. I almost felt bad for the guy until I remembered he was all of those things.

I stubbornly stood until he disembarked two stations later. Then I sunk into my seat and allowed myself to feel miserable again.

"Don't worry, Madame," a smiling businessman said as he got off the train. "We're not all *connards*. Bonne journée."

---

[9] By now you're probably really impressed with my fluent French. Rest assured, it didn't come out as eloquently as I've represented above. But no one wants to read a bunch of broken sentences, plus, gauging the reactions of my fellow passengers, my point was coming through loud and clear, if not grammatically correct.

24

Nosy Neighbors

PARIS EXPERIENCED AN INDIAN SUMMER that fall, and so each night when Mika and I returned home from picking Leo up at the *crèche*, all the kids from our apartment building were playing in the courtyard.

Our building was one of six similar structures behind a gate with a code. Once through the gate, the first two buildings merged to form the two-story arch on which our apartment sat. Walking through the arch, you arrived at the courtyard with the park, surrounded by four buildings. Each building had seven floors and an elevator. I was dying to know if their elevators were as wacky as ours, but you needed a separate code to enter each building and I didn't want to sneak in like a creep. We had plenty of those already.

The rectangular courtyard was lined with trees and greenery, and park benches dotted the interior. I suppose calling it a park is a bit much, but I needed to somehow justify the price we were paying.

As open, green spaces are hard to come by in Paris, this residence was highly sought-after by parents. Therefore, the buildings were disproportionately populated with kids. If you didn't have kids, it would probably be hell on earth to live here. But since we had a tiny rabble-rouser of our own, we fit right in. No need to worry about him banging on pots and pans at six in the morning because the neighbor's kid had been doing it since five o' clock.

When we'd stroll in around 7:00, the courtyard would already be packed with other families: boys running or biking along the edges, girls gossiping and braiding each other's hair, and parents chatting, holding a baguette under their arm. It was like a movie set for a typical French residence—so real it was unreal.

Leo was a star from the get-go. The little girls loved him and swooned over him whenever he arrived. As I pushed the stroller to the parking garage, each girl lined up to say hello.

"Bonjour, Leo!" a four-year-old blonde cooed.

"Violette! His name is Leonardo, not Leo. Get it right," her older sister, Evangeline, scolded. "Bonjour Leonardo. Et Monsieur et Madame. Did he have a good day at the *crèche?*"

"Is he going to have a bath when he gets home?" Violette asked.

"How late does Leo get to stay up?" another of the girls, Madeleine, asked. "What's Leo's favorite food?"

I usually let Mika answer because I was too embarrassed to speak French in front of these kids. Board meetings? Yes. Kindergartners? No way. Especially not this Evangeline, who was as precocious as they come.

"Madame, are you going to have another baby?"

Yikes! How could she tell? I wasn't even showing yet.

"Eventually, yes. Why?"

"Just asking. I bet that baby will be just as adorable as Leonardo, with his beautiful long eyelashes. And what big eyes he has!"

She was starting to sound like the big, bad wolf! It would be scary if it weren't so cute.

"Madame, you're the American mom, right?"

"Oui." I guess they'd been talking about me?

"My mom doesn't like Madeleine's mom but I think she likes you. At least, I haven't heard her say anything about you. But I'll let you know."

Looks like gossip started young around here. I'm sure Evangeline's mom would be less than pleased to find out she'd been running her yap about who she did and didn't like. I made a mental note to watch what I said around this one. You never know what kids will repeat.

After my parents divorced, my mom moved to Los Angeles with my brother and me, while my dad moved to Long Island. You couldn't get any further apart geographically while still being in the continental U.S. But as they were both engineers in the aeronautics industry, only a few cities offered jobs in their field.

One evening, on our way home from afterschool daycare, I remember sitting in the front seat of the car with the window down, enjoying the fresh ocean breeze. My brother, three years old at the time, was conspicuously quiet in the backseat. As a five-year-old chatterbox, this didn't bother me one bit because I was able to talk my mom's ear off the entire ride home[10].

When we pulled up to our house, Mom and I hopped out of the car but Stephen remained in the back seat. Head

---

[10] We had developed an ingenious system for avoiding daily arguments about who got to sit in the front seat – I got the odd days and Stephen got the even ones. Even at age five, I knew I had a slight advantage, but I didn't let him know that I actually got seven more days than him each year.

down, his mop of nearly white blond hair covered his baby blue eyes. What was he up to?

"Stephen? C'mon, what's the holdup?" my mom asked through the open window.

"Nothing."

"Then will you please get out of the car and come inside?"

"No."

"Why not?"

"Because then you'll find out what I did."

What had my brother done? My mind raced with possibilities. He was notorious for keeping rocks and crayons in his pockets, which my mom never discovered until after they'd been run through the wash and ruined all the laundry. He also had a fascination with bugs and worms. Anything could be waiting for us in the backseat.

"What did you do Stephen?" My mom's voice was approaching I-just-saw-a-spider-level hysteria.

Oooh, he was going to get it good.

She opened the car door and saw a huge wad of gum stuck to the upholstery. "Stephen! I told you a hundred times not to chew gum! This is why! It makes a sticky mess that's impossible to clean up. Where did you even get the gum? Oh Stephen, I'm so disappointed in you."

"I know, Mom," he said, sounding truly pitiful. "I'm an asshole."

My mom paused for a second.

My eyes widened. I may have only been five years old but I knew that word meant something bad.

Then Mom started cracking up. "Come on, honey. Don't worry about it. We'll clean it up later. You're not an asshole. Just don't chew gum anymore, OK? And don't say that word, either."

⌘

A few weeks later, Mika and I bought a new stroller. Leo was a solid 14-month-old chunk and the walk home from the *crèche* was nearly all uphill. While Leo toddled around quite well, we couldn't expect him to make the entire 20-minute journey on foot. Heck, I hardly wanted to myself after a long day of work.

We opted for a light umbrella stroller instead of the 4x4 off-road vehicle we'd been using thus far. Leo noticed the difference and sat in it like a throne. He was oddly proud of his new wheels. We would have gone for the cheap one all along if we had known he was going to be this happy about it.

"Bonjour Leonardo! How are you today?" Evangeline greeted us, as usual, in the courtyard.

"He's great," Mika replied.

"Wow, did you get a new stroller? Nice."

How did she notice that? Sure, it looked different from our old one but judging by how crowded the parking garage was, there must have been at least 30 other strollers in the building. Did she have a notebook where she tracked each family's stroller? That sounded like something I would have done at her age.

In fact, I saw a lot of myself in this girl. She was polite, loved talking to adults, and noticed everything about everyone. If I found out she was a math geek, I might have to adopt her.

"Madame, I've been meaning to ask you. Since you're American, what language do you speak with Leonardo? English or French?"

"I speak English with him."

"And Monsieur?"

"I speak French with him," Mika said.

"And what language does Leonardo speak?"

"He hasn't started talking yet, but he will speak both French and English. Probably more French at first since that's what he hears most often." Except for Mama singing

Journey. This kid would be fluent in French and "Don't Stop Believing" in no time.

"Won't that be confusing for him?"

"That's part of why he doesn't speak yet. Bilingual children tend to start talking later. But he'll catch up, don't worry."

"Good. I *was* a little worried. I can't wait to talk to him!"

She was about four years older than Leo. The same age difference as Mika and me.

Yep, this girl was the spittin' image of me. If Baby #2 turned out to be a girl, maybe she'd be just like Evangeline. Lord help the world.

25

Père Noël Is Coming to Town

DESPITE MY BATTLES WITH NAUSEA and jerkwads on the Métro, the first three months of my second pregnancy flew by. Of course, it helped that I didn't even know I was pregnant for the first month.

Before long, Christmas decorations lined the streets of the City of Light and you could feel the holiday spirit in the air. That's something I love about France—they're tolerant of all religions but when December rolls around they squeeze Christmas decorations in every nook and cranny they can find. Political-correctness be damned.

"What would Leo like for Christmas this year?" my mom asked over the phone.

"Oh, I don't know. He already has way more than he needs and you know the Lesages are going to spoil him rotten."

"Well I'm his grandma, too! I want to spoil him!"

I was worried about receiving an overwhelming amount of gifts that would fill our overcrowded apartment to overflowing. Plus, we would have limited suitcase space on our upcoming trip to the U.S., now that we were packing for three.

"Maybe you can deposit money into his bank account?" I suggested.

We'd opened a bank account for Leo soon after he was born, which entailed even more paperwork than is typical for the French, since each parent had to sign 56 pages of mumbo jumbo.

It was worth it, not only to start my son's savings early but to receive his bank statement in the mail each month, addressed to "Monsieur Leonardo Lesage." I realize that's just French for "Mister Leonardo Lesage" but it still sounds cool. It seems so official for someone who still poops his pants.

"Mommy, could you please pass my earnings statement? I'd like to see how much interest I've accrued. And then I'll need a diaper change. It's a big one."

Clearly I'm easy to please if baby bank statements give me the giggles.

"Sure, I can deposit money into his account," my mom said. "But I want to give him fun stuff, too."

"Maybe you can stock him up on toys to keep at your house? He'll need something to play with when we come to see you in January."

"Ooh, great idea! I'm gonna take Doug shopping today."

One set of grandparents down, two to go.

Dad and Marsha were less worrisome since they'd be flying into St. Louis from Florida and wouldn't have much room in their luggage. If Leo's gifts could fit in their suitcases, then surely they could fit in ours.

So I only had to worry about Mika's parents (and aunts and uncles and grandparents). Not that I didn't want my son to have new toys and books and whatnot. I just didn't want him to be spoiled. However, since Leo was Gilbert and Catherine's first grandchild, they couldn't help themselves. Every week when I unpacked the groceries, there'd be all sorts of toys and games amongst the ~~hot dogs and chips~~ asparagus and Brussels sprouts. If this was what happened on a weekly basis, there would surely be an avalanche of gifts under the tree this Christmas. The horror!

"How does this sound?" Mika asked one night after picking Leo up from the *crèche*. "Pumpkin soup, smoked salmon, zucchini au gratin, and tiramisu."

"Exquisite. Is that what you're preparing for dinner tonight?" We didn't have any of the ingredients so I was doubtful.

"No, sorry. It's what Leo had at the *crèche* today for Christmas lunch."

"Are you serious? I had a baloney sandwich. This kid eats better than me!"

"I know! I'm jealous."

Our *crèche* had really outdone themselves. Not only were they sure to never repeat the same fruit, vegetable, or meat in one week, but they'd whipped up this masterpiece? We needed to hire Chef to prepare our own dinners.

Occurrences like this reminded me why I loved my adopted country.

"Christmas is a few days away!" I said, giddy with excitement. "What kind of cookies do you want to leave out for Santa?"

Mika stared back at me blankly.

"You know… how we leave out milk and cookies for Santa Claus on Christmas Eve?"

Still no clue.

"I know Leo is a bit young but it's an excuse for us to eat cookies!"

"Sorry," he said, snapping out of it. "I was confused. In France we leave out carrots and water. For the reindeer."

No wonder the French are so skinny.

If that was the tradition in the U.S., not only would we likely have less of an obesity problem, but I might not have ever figured out Santa wasn't real.

Each Christmas Stephen and I would faithfully set out cookies and milk, selecting different treats each year so that Santa wouldn't get bored.

"Should we give him Oreos or Pitter Patters?" I asked my four-year-old brother one holiday season.

He pondered the question with the seriousness it deserved. "We got Oreos last year. What about Chips Ahoy? They're the yummiest!"

"Yeah! Mommy, can you please buy Chips Ahoy for Santa?" I asked.

"Sure, honey."

Except she didn't. 'Twas the night before Christmas and all through the house, not a Chips Ahoy was in sight, nor Nestle Tollhouse.

"Mommy, what's this?" I asked, eyeing the plate of Fig Newtons set out next to a glass of water.

"I thought Santa might want something different this year. He'll like it, you'll see."

Nobody liked Fig Newtons except Mom. And water? Who preferred water with cookies when you had the choice of milk? Except for Mom.

Wait a minute…

At six years old, I wasn't 100% positive about my assumption. Plus, I didn't want to sabotage my chance of getting gifts if there really was a Santa Claus. I decided to play along, just to be safe.

The next morning, bountiful presents were packed

under the Christmas tree. Whew, Santa had come after all.

But then I discovered a second clue. "Mommy, Santa Claus has the same handwriting as you," I said, pointing to a gift tag.

"What a coincidence!"

"And he liked Fig Newtons and water, just like you."

"Well isn't that funny!"

"Yes, that is funny." I was on to her but didn't want to ruin Stephen's fun.

But he was on to her, too. "Wait a minute, Mommy. Are YOU Santa Claus?"

She was caught red-handed.

If only we had set out carrots and water for the "reindeer," we kids would have never been the wiser. Because if there's one thing Mom likes more than Fig Newtons (and one thing even more boring than Fig Newtons), it's carrot sticks.

ঔ৽৵

We spent Christmas Eve at Mika's parents' house, opting to set out neither cookies nor carrots since we'd be stuffing our faces at the holiday dinner.

As expected, Leo was showered with gifts from Père Noël. Mika's sister, Adeline, was also Leo's godmother and therefore brought extra gifts. Even her new boyfriend arrived with a sack full of presents.

Leo was in heaven. He could hardly decide where to begin. But once he found the loudest toy (miniature pots and pans from Ikea), he banged on them for two hours straight. Thank you, Adeline.

The next day, while Leo was taking a nap and visions of sugar plums danced in his head, Mika and I organized his toys.

Mika packed a box of the more babyish items to be saved for Baby #2. I bagged up toys for charity. We recycled the books with torn pages.

But we were still left with a mound of gifts. We didn't have room for all these toys in our apartment and we were also concerned it would give Leo sensory overload.

We further divided the toys, planning to stash them in the basement and rotate his selection on a monthly basis.

"I'll take them down," I offered.

"No, no, I'll do it," Mika countered. "No way am I letting my pregnant wife carry boxes down three flights of stairs. They'll arrest me for spousal abuse."

"OK, but I'll organize it afterward."

"Deal."

Mika was great for brute strength but when it came to organizing, I was the master. I was just pondering starting a spreadsheet when Mika returned from the basement.

"OK, all set," he said.

"Great, I'll be back soon," I said, heading downstairs to the *cave*.

Most Parisian apartment buildings have a *cave* (pronounced "kahv," which sounds way cooler than just "cave") but not every tenant is guaranteed a storage unit. And if you are lucky enough to score one, the cave is usually so creepy you wouldn't even want to use it.

In previous apartments, I rarely had the nerve to enter the cave, and never without Mika. These caves were like a scene from *The Goonies* except without the pirate treasure. Bare dirt floors, ominous shadows, suspicious squeaky noises, and a distinctive musty odor.

Half-convinced I would stumble across a skeleton with a whisky bottle, I always dashed in and out as quickly as possible, then immediately hopped in the shower to rid myself of the inevitable cobwebs stuck in my hair.

This cave, though, had concrete floors and was swept often. The low ceilings and occasional spider reminded you it was still a basement, but I could handle being down there by myself without freaking out. Our storage unit even had its own light!

I settled in to Operation Organization. Since this was our fifth apartment together, Mika and I had discarded a lot of crap on each previous move. The storage unit contained only luggage, seasonal items, and a stash of newborn clothes sealed in bags. But Leo's new toys would fill up half the space. If we were going to stick to our plan of rotating them out on a regular basis, they needed to be part of an organized system. (I really should have gone for the spreadsheet.)

When I finished, I backed out of the storage unit, ready to head upstairs. But outside of the storage unit, the cave was pitch black.

Crap! The overhead light must have been on a timer. The light from our storage unit was bright, but not quite bright enough to reach around the corner to the stairwell where the main light switch was. I'd have to venture into the dark to flip it on.

All of a sudden, the cave seemed a lot scarier. Every zombie movie I'd ever watched popped into my head. When you're sitting on your couch it's easy to shout, "Just stab him in the brain, dummy! What's the big deal?"

But now that a zombie could jump out of a corner at any moment, I realized it wasn't quite so easy. I could probably take a child zombie or maybe another woman. But what if the zombie was a tall man? How would I reach high enough to stab him in the head? Especially since my only weapon was my set of keys?

I ran as fast as I could to the stairwell and hit the light. Whew, no zombies.

I casually strolled back to the storage unit like the cool Zombie Slayer I was. Who's not afraid of zombies now? Now that the light is on.

I flipped off the switch in our storage unit and locked up before the overhead light had a chance to kick off again. Not that I was afraid of zombies. I just wanted to get upstairs before my son woke up from his nap.

Yeah, that was it.

26

U.S. Bound

WITH THE HOLIDAY SEASON BEHIND US, we packed up the Christmas tree and hauled out the luggage for our trip to the U.S. I sent Mika down to the Zombie Cave, having not fully recovered from my last basement adventure.

International flights are never easy, but with a 17-month-old they are a true test of your patience. I didn't need a test because I already knew my results: I had zero patience.

Fortunately, our curious little boy actually behaved himself during the 9 1/2 hour flight to Chicago. He found an empty cabinet near our seat (thank you, plane interior designers!) and contented himself with opening it, smiling at us, closing it, smiling at us, and repeating for about three hours.

At one point, a passenger ran past him, threw up on the floor, and then fainted. This provided an additional hour of interest for Leo, and even though I knew I should give the man some privacy, I thought it would be better for everyone on the plane if my son was occupied, albeit by gawking at a stranger's misfortune.

Also, as someone who had thrown up on a plane before, I was curious to see it from the other perspective. Hey, it's a long flight. How else are you going to pass the time?

"Welcome to Chicago, where the temperature is -11 degrees. We touched down on time, but we'll be waiting on the tarmac for a few minutes here due to the weather."

No problem, I could handle a few minutes. The trip had gone surprisingly smoothly up to that point, with no crying (from me or Leo) and now here we were on time!

Two hours later, we were still waiting on the tarmac. The brutally low temperatures meant the airport employees could only be outside for five-minute intervals, thus causing a monumental backup in directing planes to their gates, setting up jet bridges, and unloading luggage.

Our fellow passengers panicked at the delay, but I was cool as a cucumber. "Don't worry, Mika. There are flights from Chicago to St. Louis every hour so even if we miss ours, we can catch the next one. Worst case, we can always drive." I laughed. "Though I'd be surprised if it came to that."

Once we were set free, passengers clawed over each other to escape. The mass of humanity headed up the jetway, where a somber-faced gate agent directed us to a wall pinned with tickets for rebooked flights. I doubted ours would be up there but checked anyway.

ST. LOUIS-LESAGE screamed at me beneath a skull and crossbones sketched on the front of the envelope.

Why were *we* being rebooked? Hopefully it was for the next flight.

I opened the envelope to discover that we'd been rebooked for two days later.

"Mika, this is outrageous! We're rebooked for Wednesday!"

Mika's face fell while Leo glanced around for some trouble to cause. "I'm not staying in freezing ass Chicago for two days. I want to visit your family!"

"Screw this. We're driving. It's only about five hours."

But before we could leave we had to go through passport control, retrieve our bags, then pass through customs. And of course I couldn't get a signal on my cell phone so I couldn't book a car yet.

"We need to change Leo's diaper," I said while we waited at the baggage carousel. "And I really need to pee." I was five months pregnant and was shocked I hadn't already peed my pants. I normally could only hold it about thirty minutes.

"OK, I'll stay here and wait for the bags," Mika offered.

I hustled Leo to the bathroom where the world's longest line greeted me. Crap. We needed to snag a rental car before the rest of the airport had the same idea. I couldn't afford to wait an hour.

"Back so soon?" Mika asked, still no luggage.

"The line reached all the way to hell. I'll just hold it and I guess Leo's fine for now."

The bags trundled out an hour later. If I'd have known it would take that long, I would have waited for the bathroom!

We breezed through customs and were greeted by an airline representative.

"How can I help you?" he asked.

"Hi, sir. We are rebooked on a flight for Wednesday but we live close enough to drive. If we skip this leg of our trip is the rest of our ticket still valid?"

I wanted to verify this before we blew $2,000 worth of international travel, especially since I'd heard airlines invalidate the rest of your flight if you miss a leg. Apparently it's to deter people from booking a cheaper round-trip flight when they're only planning to use one portion.

"You'll have to ask an agent in Terminal 3."

"Which terminal are we in?"

"Five. You have to take the tram to Terminal 3. Except the tram isn't working because of the cold. But there should be a bus running. Head out these double doors here, then follow the crowd."

Mika took the luggage while I handled the stroller and our carry-ons. We waited patiently by the exit, freezing our noses off every time the automatic doors opened. Minus 11 degrees was bad enough, but the arctic wind chill dropped it to 25 below zero. Leo started to cry, probably from a combination of stress, hunger, and the cold. Great.

A bus with a sign taped to the side, on which was scrawled Terminal 3, pulled up across the street. A horde of people scrambled out of the building, climbing over each other to board. The bus drove away with doors open and people hanging off the back, leaving a crowd on the curb that looked just as large as the initial crowd.

Were these people going to wait outside for the next bus? My asthmatic son surely wouldn't be able to last more than a minute, and honestly, neither could I. My contacts would freeze to my eyeballs. How would we ever get on the bus? There would always be a group of people more desperate than us who'd endure the cold to ensure they got on the next bus.

We weren't making it to Terminal 3.

I whipped out my phone and searched for a signal while Mika tended to a crying Leo.

"Mom? It's me. Not much time to talk. We're stuck in Chicago until Wednesday unless I can get a car out of here. Could you—"

"Wednesday! But I want to see my grandbaby!"

"Mom, no time. And don't you want to see us, too? Never mind, no time. Can you please call the airline and check to see if we void our tickets by driving this leg instead of flying? I'm going to try to rent a car. I'll call you back in five."

I hung up before she could ask how Leo was doing. We had to hurry, even if it meant being rude to my mom for a few minutes. She would understand.

I spotted a bank of ancient telephones with signs overhead advertising hotels and car rental agencies. Bingo.

"Mika, I'm going over there to call the car rental place. You got Leo?"

"Yep!" Leo had settled down but was still clearly out of his element. The airport was frigid, the bottle Mika had tried to give him was cold, and I'm sure his diaper was nice and warm. But what could we do? The entire airport was crowded, making it impossible to go to the bathroom or heat a baby bottle in under an hour, and we needed to be ready to dash off at a moment's notice.

The phone area was utter chaos. One phone was broken and the others were occupied. Two groups were ahead of me—a pair of college-aged girls and a family of four—but the rest were a scattered mess of idiots. Some were checking the arrivals screen above the hotel ads, others were drifting aimlessly. All of them stood between me and my escape route—the phones—and so they all posed a threat.

I tried to keep cool but some moron butted in front of me. It was bad enough I had to wait while cars were being snatched from beneath my nose, but I sure as heck wasn't going to let somebody cut in line.

In France, where situations like this happen on a daily basis, I control my rage because it's not my country and not my language. I don't want to be the crazy foreigner shouting in broken French at a bunch of strangers.

But we were in my country now and my compatriots were acting like a bunch of fools. I couldn't take it anymore.

"People, people!" I shouted. "This madness has to

stop. Who's in line? Raise your hand."

The crowd turned to look at the shouting crazy lady but no one raised their hand.

"I mean business, folks. I need to get my family out of this hellhole and this pathetic excuse for a line isn't helping. Raise your hand if you're in line or else you just lost your place."

Blank stares.

"Alright, I'll do it for you. You two," I said, pointing at the college girls. "You're next. After you is this family. Then it's me. If anyone else even tries to butt in front of me, I will murder you."

A petite redhead meekly held up her hand. "Um, I was in line too."

"OK, then step right up. Though you might want to reconsider your definition of a line." I looked around for any other issues. "You, sir. Are you waiting for the phones?"

A clueless Asian guy turned around. "Um, I watch screen."

"Excellent. Step to the left and you can look as long as you like. Anyone else checking the monitors? Step to the left! I want one straight line for the phones. Got it?"

People queued up behind me while the stragglers pulled over to the side to check the arrivals screen. Was that so hard?

As I waited in my military-precision line, I remembered I needed to call Mom back.

"Hi honey, how's it going?"

"I yelled at half the airport, I have to pee, and Leo is on the verge of a breakdown. But Mika is holding it together. One out of three ain't bad." I waved over at my husband and son. "How about you? Did you get a hold of the airline?"

"Yep, and I did you one better. First, the airline said it's no problem for you to drive. You just have to call them later to reconfirm your tickets."

No problem, we could do that once we were safe and sound in St. Louis. "Thanks. And what's the other thing?"

"Doug booked you a car with Hertz. You just have to find a bus to take you to their lot and give them this confirmation number. You have a pen?"

With my phone (and patience) cutting in and out, it took a few tries to note the impossibly long confirmation number, but I got it. "Thank you both so much. Oh shoot, I see a Hertz bus pulling up. Gotta go!"

I ran over to Mika, leaving my perfectly formed line of people wondering why I'd made such a fuss only to leave two seconds later. Screw 'em.

"Mika, we gotta catch that bus. Go, go!"

He'd been holding Leo to keep him calm and I knew we wouldn't have time to buckle him back in and still make the bus. If Leo doesn't want to be in the stroller, he does The Plank and remains stick-straight so that there's no way to wedge him in without breaking his legs.

Mika ran with Leo in one arm, dragging a suitcase with the other. I tossed the carry-ons into the stroller, pushing it with one hand (which caused it to veer wildly out of control), while dragging the other suitcase behind me.

The sidewalk and road were icy and the bitter cold air froze me to the bone the second I got outside. Mika made it on the bus, which was on the other side of the road, but I still had about 50 feet to cover. It's hard for a five-months-pregnant lady to run very fast on ice, particularly when weighed down by bags.

"Wait! Wait!" I shouted. The bus started to drive away with my husband and son on it, but the doors were still open. "Wait you *bleep-er bleepin'* bus! I'm five *bleeping* months pregnant and my *bleeping* family is on that *bleeping* bus!"

After my eloquent speech, the bus driver stopped. I tossed the luggage and stroller on and flew up the stairs.

"Good evening, everyone," I said with a smile,

smoothing my hair. "Thank you for waiting," I said to the bus driver.

"Nice move, Mama," Mika said. "I was afraid he was going to leave without you! I tried to get him to stop but I guess he didn't hear me."

Well, he—and the entire airport—certainly heard *me*!

༄ঌ

The bus arrived at the car rental lot. We were almost on our way.

Due to the severe cold, all the cars in the lot were already turned on. So wasteful, so American, so helpful. Because otherwise the doors would freeze shut and render the cars unusable.

A few papers to sign and we'd be *en route*. I chitchatted with the guy at the desk while Mika installed the car seat. I commended the Hertz employee for braving the cold and working in such crappy weather. Their outpost was heated with only one dinky space heater and they didn't even have a bathroom. Which sucked for me and my full bladder but must have really sucked for them.

"So where do you guys go to the bathroom?"

"We have to walk across the lot to the main office."

"In this cold?"

Right then Mika burst through the door. "I'm sorry but I can't figure out the car seat. And my feet are frozen." His thin Converse shoes didn't stand up against the snow and freezing temperatures.

"I'll help you sir," the desk agent volunteered. In France they would have said "That's not our job," and sat behind the desk drinking coffee while you slowly lost one limb after another to frostbite.

Soon enough, we were on our way. Leo, his diaper weighing more than him now, passed out immediately in the back seat.

"Here we go!" I cheered, pulling out of the lot. "It's normally about five hours to St. Louis, but since we're already outside the city, it might even be faster!"

It wasn't.

The roads were paved in slick ice, and roadside notification boards urged travelers to "Only travel if necessary. Roads in dangerous condition."

I averaged about 40 miles per hour, taking cues from the truckers on the road. If I saw their brakes light up in the distance ahead, I had ample time to slow down before hitting the rough patch. If they were sailing smoothly, I allowed myself to accelerate to the luxurious speed of 60 miles per hour. At this rate, the journey would take seven hours. Add in the time difference with Paris and it would feel like driving until 9 am.

"We should stop for coffee," I suggested. "Plus Mama needs to pee."

"You don't have to tell me twice!" Mika said.

Here's the thing I love about America (apart from my Hertz Hero): We were in the middle of a snowstorm and the lowest temperatures the Chicago area had seen in 30 years, yet the gas stations were open with freshly brewed coffee and fresh-enough donuts. The bathrooms were decently clean and didn't cost a dime.

We took turns running into the shop, not wanting to wake Leo up or remove him from the warmth of the car. That also meant we missed another opportunity for a diaper change. If I wasn't careful, I'd get pulled over for being the world's worst parent.

❦

"Isn't that the saddest story you've ever heard?" I said, wiping the tears from my eyes.

Two coffee breaks later, we were about 30 minutes away from my mom's house. We'd passed the long hours by telling embarrassing stories from our younger days, and then somehow I got on the subject of how *The Time Traveler's Wife* was the best yet saddest book I'd ever read. So sad that I brought myself to tears just talking about it.

I really needed to sleep.

Right about then, my precious angel in the back seat woke up. I couldn't believe he'd made it that long. Poor guy had had a rough 24 hours. And now he was pissed off.

"What should we do, Mika? We have to keep him in his car seat. You want to try feeding him?"

"From the front?"

"Can you hop in the back?"

"While we're driving?"

"I really don't want to stop if we don't have to. It's already 1:30 in the morning. I just want to get home. We're almost there."

My 6'4" husband squeezed between the seats and landed on the back seat as gracefully as a drunk on a banana peel. He tried to give Leo a cold bottle. No dice. Seconds later, cookies flew past me and landed on the dashboard. I guess he didn't want those either.

"The wheels on the bus go round and round, round and round," I started. Leo instantly calmed. Great! I could do this the rest of the ride if I had to!

I had to.

Thirty minutes later we pulled into my parents' driveway as I sung the last made-up chorus of the song I now hated. "The mommy in the car is going crazy, going crazy, going crazy!"

Mom rushed out in her pajamas to greet us while Doug unloaded our luggage.

"You made it!" she said, giving us hugs and kisses. "Now let me see my sweet grandson."

"No problem. First order of business—you can change his diaper."

27

Heartbreaker, Noisemaker

IT WAS GREAT TO BE BACK in the U.S. We indulged in all sorts of American delicacies, like triple cheeseburgers and double-chocolate milkshakes. Leo played in the snow for the first time. And Mika and I got to relax while Mom fed, bathed, and entertained our son.

This pregnancy seemed way harder than my first, and the grueling 24-hour journey to St. Louis hadn't helped. I enjoyed lounging in the recliner, watching Leo and Grandma and Grandpa play with their new toys. Let's be honest—considering how often Doug played "Twinkle, Twinkle, Little Star" on the xylophone, I'm pretty sure he got it for himself. And Mom never tired of stacking blocks for Leo to knock down.

One of the most exciting parts of the trip was finding out the gender of Baby #2. While my official medical appointments were required to be within the French healthcare system, nothing prevented us from having a vanity ultrasound in the U.S.

Mom had scheduled an appointment at a place that screamed American capitalism. I couldn't have been happier. Their website promised a "gender reveal," as well as a DVD with 2D and 3D images.

But that's not all! The Gender Reveal Package came with a Heartbeat Teddy Bear, where the baby's heartbeat was recorded on a little device inside a pink or blue bear.

"Can we order extra?" I'd asked my mom after she booked the date. "I definitely need more than one. I can't believe I've gone my whole life without a heartbeat teddy bear." I wasn't joking. Have you heard of anything cooler?

"Yes, you can purchase an extra one for $25."

God bless America. They sure know how to make a buck.

On the day of the ultrasound, Mom, Doug, Mika, Leo and I piled into the car.

"What's everyone's guess on the gender?" Mom asked.

"Girl," I said. "But that's just because it's what I'm hoping for."

"Girl," Doug said. "I have a feeling."

"Boy," Mika said. "And I hope he's a carbon copy of Leo. Leo is so perfect, I want another one just like him!"

"I think it will be a girl," Mom said. "That way I have one grandbaby of each gender."

We'd find out soon enough!

As we entered the three-story brick office complex, a couple with a blue teddy bear and frowns on their faces nearly knocked us over on their way out. Looked like someone wasn't happy about the gender of their baby. How sad! Even though I said I wanted a girl, I would be happy with either[11].

Pushing open the door to Exciting and Expensive

---

[11] Many people say this and then add "as long as the baby is healthy." Is that really necessary? Does anyone want one gender so badly that they would wish for an unhealthy baby as long as they got their preferred gender? Obviously I want a healthy baby, dummies.

Ultrasounds, we were greeted with a warm and welcoming suite. That's what you get when you spring for a superfluous gender reveal, as opposed to a routine medical visit.

We settled in on the plush leather sofa until the technician appeared.

"Mrs. Lesage?" A perky woman about my age peeked her head around the door to the ultrasound room. "My name is Amy. Come on in! And your family is welcome to join, or they can watch on the screen in the waiting room."

Everyone opted to join me. As I was five months pregnant, the bump was prominent enough that I wouldn't have to pull my pants down and embarrass anyone during the procedure.

For once, I got to keep my clothes on.

"I'm so excited!" Mom said. "I've never seen an ultrasound before. That technology wasn't common when I had my babies."

"Are you calling me old?" I asked. "Because if I'm old, remember you're 25 years older."

She also figured this would be her only chance to experience an ultrasound, since Stephen and his wife, Nikki, lived in Michigan. If they had a baby someday, Mom probably wouldn't fly out of state for the appointment.

"We didn't have ultrasounds with Justin and Eric, either," Doug said, which made sense since my step-brothers were roughly the same age as Stephen and me. "I'm excited, too!"

In fact we all were, which is more than I can say for when we found out Leo's gender.

I'm normally an on-time person. In fact, I usually arrive early to avoid the stress and sweat that comes from running late.

But for the second-trimester ultrasound with Baby #1, Mika and I were three minutes late. Three ghastly, horrible, reprehensible minutes.

At least that's what the doctor would have had us believe.

For our first ultrasound, we had the best doctor in the world. He literally whistled while he worked and was one of the most charming Frenchmen I've ever met (besides Mika, of course).

However, he retired a few weeks after our appointment. His assistant recommended another doctor and we assumed he would be just as good.

Nope.

Medically speaking I suppose he was fine. But he had absolutely no bedside manner whatsoever.

"Madame Lesage, you are late. Fill out these forms," Dr. Ivry barked.

I split the ginormous stack with Mika to speed up the process. We completed the paperwork in record time and were back on track.

"Sit over there and let's get started."

Yes sir!

He glided the wand over my protruding belly, not even bothering to point out our baby's features. He muttered words like "bladder" and "very good" but I would have liked a play-by-play. I understood he had a schedule to keep, but three minutes late, particularly in France, is nothing. And surely we'd made up the time by now. Couldn't he slow down?

"Vertebral column, good. Ten toes, good. Do you want to know the sex?"

The moment we'd been waiting for!

I had felt all along that Baby #1 would be a girl. Mika and I had chosen a boy's name just in case but we'd already pictured a girl in our minds. Here was the moment of truth.

"It's a boy. Ten fingers, good. Heartbeat, good."

I turned to Mika and we both had tears in our eyes. I was happy to know the gender of my baby because I could now call it "him." But Dr. Ivry had blurted it so quickly that I felt cheated of the fun. It was also not the news I was expecting (even though it was foolish to have ever thought I knew my baby's gender beforehand) so I was a little thrown off.

He concluded the appointment as brusquely as it had begun and thrust several print-outs in my hand.

"Bonne journée, and don't be late next time."

"Ready?" The ultrasound technician in the cozy St. Louis office smiled as she squeezed gel on my belly. "Sorry, it's a bit cold."

I'm pretty sure "sorry" wasn't even in Dr. Ivry's vocabulary.

As the first image flashed on the screen, I looked over at my family waiting in the chairs. Well, Mom, Doug, and Mika were seated. Leo was already off exploring the room, seeing what kind of trouble he could get into.

My parents and husband had tears in the corners of their eyes. Awww.

Amy announced each body part as it popped up on the screen. Head, eyes, spine, bladder. Some parts were easy to identify but some weren't as easy to spot, especially for Mom and Doug who were seeing grainy ultrasound images for the first time.

Amy switched the screen to 3D. Mika and I had been afraid it would be creepy but it was amazing. We could see our baby's face! How cute!

"And I assume you want to find out the gender today?"

"Yes!" Mom and I shouted.

"It looks like you'll be having a girl!"

Now the waterworks really kicked in. All of us adults

welled up and Leo stopped tugging on a lamp cord to see why it had suddenly gone quiet. He saw me crying and ran over to the side of the bed and leaned his head against my hand. He was a guy's guy—always smashing or pulling on something—but he was a sweetie, too.

"OK, now for the heartbeat." Amy pulled out a heart-shaped recording device and pressed the audio button on the ultrasound machine.

Whomp, whomp, whomp.

"Woo-woo-woo!" Leo chimed in, slapping the bed. He was back to his brute self.

"I'll have to try that one again," Amy said, with no hint of frustration at my son having ruined her recording.

It took seven attempts to capture two clear recordings without Leo adding his own soundtrack. She placed the hearts into the teddy bears and handed me my pricy yet priceless treasures.

"Best of luck with the rest of your pregnancy. And enjoy your baby girl!"

28

Rush Hour Stops for No One

"I DON'T WANT TO LEAVE!" I whined to my mom in the airport check-in line. She and Doug had parked the car and walked us in to say goodbye, a huge change from previous airport drop-offs where Mom barely slowed down the car before pushing me out the door. It's not that she didn't love me, it's that she didn't like change and for some reason or another we'd always done airport drop-offs that way.

Now, though, with a cuddly grandson to bid adieu to, she had the kick in the butt she needed to learn how the parking garage at Lambert St. Louis International Airport worked.

"I know, honey. I'm going to miss you all so much."

Turns out we had plenty more time together, thanks to the dingbat working at the check-in counter.

"OK, let's see here. Mr. and Mrs. Lesage. Plus an infant. And that's St. Louis, Chicago, Paris. Now, which flight is first?" The agent scratched his full head of gray hair while looking directly at me.

Wait, was he serious? We were currently in St. Louis, flying through Chicago, continuing on to Paris. I would love nothing more than to go straight to Paris but that wasn't an option from the St. Louis airport, despite its international status.

"We'll be going to Chicago first, then Paris." I barely managed a straight face.

"Ah, right. That makes sense. Thanks." It took him another 30 minutes to sort out the "infant in arms" situation since Leo was young enough to not require a paid ticket but still needed a boarding pass. "I'm sorry, ma'am. I'm old and I'm slow. Let me ask my colleague for help."

I could hardly criticize him when he'd summed it up so well himself, so I used the delay as an opportunity to enjoy a few more minutes with Mom and Doug before heading overseas.

"We'll visit as soon as that baby is born!" Mom said.

"Looking forward to it. Plan for some time in May."

❧

One thing I was not looking forward to was going back to work. It'd been so nice to lounge in my parents' living room all day, watching Leo interact with his grandparents. No daily grind and tons of ice cream.

Now I had to return to my hour-long morning commute, grueling meeting-filled days, and hour-long evening commute. At least my belly was obvious enough that I usually got a seat on the Métro without having to ask.

When I returned to the office, I discovered that none of my colleagues had gotten anything done, despite me having organized task lists before leaving and giving my team plenty to work on. The bosses were on my case, as if it was my fault that everyone had slacked off during my two-week absence. Fun.

And I was exhausted all the time. I didn't remember it being this hard with Leo. How was I going to make it another four months until my due date?

❦

On a blustery Thursday morning, I trudged into the office as usual. The escalator in the Métro station was broken (despite having been replaced two months earlier), so I had to walk up the four flights of stairs to exit.

Then I endured meeting after meeting where management asked why we were behind, and I ended up taking the blame for every else's failures. One such fun-fest dragged on well past lunch hour. Not to be high-maintenance, but as I was growing another human inside of me, I needed to eat at regular intervals. But every attempt to steer the meeting back on track resulted in further tangents by the bosses. As if they were doing it on purpose, like some sort of power trip.

Finally, minutes before I nearly fainted and 45 minutes after we should have been allowed to leave, we were released. I stuffed my face and felt better, then somehow managed to finish the rest of my work day.

For a country that's great at slacking off, they sure hadn't given this pregnant lady any breaks. Which normally wouldn't bother me—I had a strong work ethic and got great satisfaction out of completing projects.

Why was I so run down, especially right after a vacation?

❦

The next day, I worked from home because my monthly check-up at the hospital was scheduled for smack dab in the middle of the day. Spending a total of four hours commuting would be pointless and I'd accomplish much more at home.

Or so I thought.

You see, this was the routine appointment where they discovered I was already four centimeters dilated. That doesn't sound like much, especially since few Americans know what the heck a centimeter is, but considering 10 centimeters means you're ready to give birth, four is kind of a big deal.

Add in the contractions coming every two minutes and I was certain I was going to deliver my baby at 25 weeks and 3 days.

"Just because you're in preterm labor doesn't mean you'll deliver your baby today," the tall, handsome OB/GYN reassured me.

Yeah, right. That's what they'd said about Leo and he ended up being born that day (well, technically after midnight but still within 24 hours of the first contraction).

"But in case your little one decides to arrive early," a sweet *sage-femme* with a brunette bob added, "we have a pediatrician on her way to discuss your options."

My options?

A thin Indian woman, who would have been pretty except for her frown, entered the room. "Hi, my name is Debbie Downer and I'm about to say a whole bunch of stuff you don't want to hear. I have no bedside manner and I'm scaring the shit out of you right now. But it's best, for your baby's sake, to remain calm."

The OB/GYN and *sage-femme* dropped their jaws.

Dr. Downer continued with information I can't even repeat here because it's heartbreaking. I was now convinced my poor baby girl would be born with all sorts of serious problems, if she was even born alive at all. Not the best way to keep me calm.

Fortunately, Debbie Downer got paged to deliver crappy news to someone else. She pulled the hood of her Grim Reaper cloak over her head and exited the room, scythe in hand.

The OB/GYN attempted some damage control in her wake. "We have to be honest and tell you your baby could be born today, but there's also a possibility she could stay in much longer. Our immediate goal is to stabilize your contractions for the next four days and get you to 26 gestational weeks, which will take you out of the scary 'Gray Zone' Dr. Downer was talking about and put you in the 'Grand Prématuré' zone. It's still risky but it's much better."

The following milestone would be 34 weeks, where the baby would simply be premature, then 37 weeks, where she would just be early, and then if everyone's thoughts and prayers worked, 39 weeks, which would be full-term.

That meant my baby girl's birthday could be in January, February, March, April or May. I didn't have time to worry about her having an odd-numbered birthdate—I didn't even know which season she'd be born in!

"We're transferring you to Port Royal because we don't have enough room here. They will take great care of you, I promise."

I found out later that the real reason I was transferred is because Maternité Port Royal specializes in babies born before 26 weeks, whereas Trousseau handles preemies born after that point. In case Baby #2 was born that weekend, they wanted me to be in the right place. Agreed, but I'm glad I didn't realize it at the time.

"An ambulance will be here shortly to transfer you," the *sage-femme* said. "Try to relax."

Relax? I'd never ridden in an ambulance before. This would be so cool! Whizzing around the streets of Paris with the siren blaring, passing other vehicles, being top priority in rush hour traffic. In a few minutes, I'd be on the ride of my life!

None of that happened.

First, we had to wait two hours for the ambulance. I

understand I wasn't in critical condition and Trousseau could care for me until my transportation showed up. It's not like I was lying in the street dying of a massive head wound. I was safe in a hospital attached to an IV with a steady drip of medicine to keep my contractions in check.

Still, it seems an ambulance should arrive at a destination in under two hours.

"Madame Lesage?" A petite blonde with one arm in a sling, an equally tiny brunette with "Trainee" marked on her badge, and an old guy with a potbelly surrounded my gurney[12]. Not to judge, but I kind of expected paramedics who looked a little more qualified to transport a patient.

They spent 10 minutes setting up the transfer gurney, Old Guy sweating and panting with exertion. Sling was in charge, explaining to Trainee how to reposition the IV and where to stash my dossier. They unzipped an insulated bag, which unnervingly resembled a body bag.

"We're ready," Sling said.

"OK, I grab feet, you grab shoulders," Old Guy said to Trainee with a strong Portuguese accent.

Trainee couldn't have weighed more than 100 pounds soaking wet. I doubted she could lift my upper torso. And Sling obviously couldn't either.

"Would you like me to help?" Mika offered. He was concerned his precious cargo might have a rough transition to the gurney.

"That's great idea," Old Guy said. "One, two, three!"

They heaved me on to the ambulance gurney, then zipped me into my body bag.

"Try to stay calm, Madame. We'll be on our way soon," Sling said.

I was remaining surprisingly chill considering I was in a body bag. The only problem was that Old Guy's huge

---

[12] Be honest, you thought I was going to say "walked into a bar." That does sound like the set up to a joke. Well, keep reading. It basically was.

potbelly hung over the gurney and pushed into my feet. I felt rude pressing on his stomach but it took a lot of effort to pull my feet away from him. In the end, safety won out over politeness and I let my feet rest on his tummy. I'm sure it wasn't the first time someone had used it as a footrest.

The team of paramedics wheeled me out while the OB/GYN and *sage-femme* waved goodbye. "Good luck, Madame. You're in good hands."

Good, maybe. Capable, not so sure.

But I had to admit, it was pretty cool. The ceilings blurred past me and doors swung open in my honor. I was a big deal.

Mika and Old Guy loaded me onto the ambulance. "I'll see you on the flip side," Mika said. "I love you." He and Old Guy headed to the front seat, while the two girls climbed into the back with me.

"Love you, too," I said, tears welling up in my eyes despite myself.

Port Royal should have been a 15 minute ride away, particularly since we were in an ambulance. But this was Paris.

You see, I was in a private ambulance since my situation wasn't that dire, and those don't have the right-of-way. I don't know how, as a driver, you can tell the difference between which ambulances get priority and which ones you can ignore, but that's information I don't ever need to know. If I were driving, I would pull over if I saw an ambulance. What if your grandmother were in there, people?

But alas, we were stuck in Friday night rush hour traffic like the other half a million Parisian commuters, despite our sirens blasting.

The paramedics made small talk, asking me about Leo and if I had a name picked out yet for Baby #2. They put me at ease and turned out to be very apt at their jobs. They may not have been able to lift anything heavier than a croissant, and I'll still never understand why you would allow a paramedic to work in a sling, but at that moment, they were keeping Mama calm, so I loved them.

After half an hour we pulled into Port Royal, where Old Guy and Mika unloaded me.

"Here's my number," Sling said, handing Mika a piece of paper. "Please let me know when your daughter is born, hopefully many weeks from now. Good luck!"

29

Five-Star Hotel

"MADAME LESAGE, I need to ask you a few questions," a young *sage-femme* instructed me. She plopped a huge dossier on the desk in the exam room and my heart skipped a beat as she flipped through the crisp, blank pages. Was she planning to fill out *all* those papers?

"I believe they transferred her dossier from Trousseau," Mika said. "Maybe you can look for that? It should have everything you need."

"I'll look for it in a minute. Let's fill this out first."

Um, no, nimwit. The whole point of finding the dossier was to avoid filling out the same paperwork twice. But I was too exhausted to argue. I just wanted to check into the new hospital (or "hotel" as I inexplicably called it over the next four days) and go to bed.

"Let's begin with your name, address, and birth date."

"I'm going to look for the dossier," Mika interrupted, leaving the room.

But the *sage-femme* continued with her inane questions,

unperturbed. "How many pregnancies have you had?"

"Two. I have a 17-month-old son and I'm 25 weeks pregnant with this one."

"OK, I'm going to begin with questions about your first pregnancy."

She asked about my general health, Leo's birth weight, and 42 other pieces of information.

"Do you smoke?"

"No."

"Drink?"

"Not while pregnant."

"OK, that wraps up the questions for the first pregnancy. Have you had any other pregnancies?"

Was she kidding? First, I already told her I had two pregnancies. Second, unless an alien was about to pop out of my tummy, some pretty strong evidence was staring her right in the face that I did, indeed, have at least one other pregnancy besides the one I just answered questions about.

"Yes."

"When?"

Oh my god. This lady was killing me!

"Right now. I'm at 25 weeks and 3 days."

She scratched it down on the paper as if hearing the information for the first time.

"OK, I'm going to ask you a few questions about your second pregnancy."

She proceeded to ask all the same questions she had asked about the first pregnancy.

"Can't you just copy the information from the form? Nothing has changed."

"The birth weight will be different."

"But my baby isn't even born yet! You'll have to leave that part blank. All the other information is the same."

"Madame, please. We need to go through this form line by line. It's the quickest way."

I begged to differ. But what else was there to do?

Besides be extremely uncomfortable. She'd sat me on an exam table and placed my feet in stirrups, even though I was not presently undergoing any examination and was fully clothed. Even if she did plan on examining me, I'd have to undress first, so it seemed my feet didn't yet need to be holstered in the stirrups.

"Before we continue, could we please adjust my position? The doctors keep telling me to take it easy but here I am straining to keep the stirrups from sliding out to the side."

She looked around the room for a solution. "I guess I could give you my stool," she offered. She slid it in between the stirrups and rested my legs on it.

Better, but it seemed like there should have been another option. Lower the part of the table my back was resting on? Pull out an extension at the foot of the table? Surely this was not standard procedure for stopping contractions. At least with her standing she might run through the questions more quickly.

Right as she asked me if I smoked, Mika and another *sage-femme*, the only chubby one I'd ever seen, walked in.

The new *sage-femme*'s eyes bugged out. "C'est quoi ce bordel?" she asked.

Literally that means "What's this brothel?" but in colloquial terms it's come to mean "What's this mess?" However, it is still a strong phrase that you wouldn't normally hear a medical professional use. Which indicated I had indeed been right—the form-completing *sage-femme* was a dummy.

"Pardonnez-nous, Madame. I am Emilie, the *sage-femme* who will be handling your check-in. Welcome to Port Royal. Now let's get you more comfortable."

With a quick flick of a switch, she lowered the head of the exam table, then inserted a padded extension at the feet. She kicked the stool away while giving the other *sage-femme* the evil eye.

"We found your dossier so you don't need to fill out the one she's been asking you."

I knew it!

"I'll do a quick exam and you'll be on your way."

I wasn't optimistic about the "quick" part—I'd heard that way too many times throughout the day and nothing had been fast—but I at least had confidence she was large and in charge.

She did an ultrasound to check how much I was dilated (No fingers? Shame.) and verified I had not dilated further but was still at a scary 37 mm.

"We will keep you in the hospital until the contractions have stabilized. Once they have, we'll take you off the medicine and as long as you don't have contractions for 24 hours, you can go home."

Worked for me. An orderly transferred me to my hotel room. "I'll be right back with your dinner," he said.

Mika kissed me on the forehead. "It looks like we made it through today. I need to pick up Leo at my parents' house. You gonna be OK?"

Heck yes! I was about to enjoy my first full night of sleep in ages. Dinner was on its way and my only command was to eat and sleep. I could do this.

"I'll be back first thing tomorrow morning and I'll bring Leo to visit. I know you miss him."

"I do. Thanks, you're the best."

∾∾

Bright and early the next morning, Mika arrived with my gorgeous son. I burst into tears as I gave them both a hug, not having spent the night apart from either of them since leaving the hospital after Leo's birth.

I know. I need to get out more.

Leo was confused about his surroundings and didn't understand why Mommy wasn't chasing him around like usual. But with plenty of wires and cords for him to play with, he got over it quickly.

"I brought everything on your list," Mika said as he unpacked my bag into the hotel closet.

Though I'd promised myself I'd be prepared this pregnancy, how could I have anticipated preterm labor at 25 weeks? I sighed. I might as well get used to being a few steps behind from now on.

My boys left not too long after, figuring they'd better get out of my hair before Leo pulled out my IV. My friends, Chris and Wooster (surprisingly, not her real name) came to visit as well, and before I knew it I'd passed another day without delivering my baby.

That night, I ate my scrumptious hotel dinner and watched the French version of "Who Wants to Be a Millionaire." As I spread creamy Brie on my baguette (see, I wasn't joking—the hotel food was delicious) I guessed along with the players.

"Who was leader of the U.S.S.R. when the Berlin Wall fell?"

Easy peasy. I knew this not only because I was a trivia buff but because I'd actually met Gorbachev when he came to none other than my home state of Missouri to deliver a speech about the end of the Cold War.

I scanned the answers for Gorby and was met with the following options: Boris Eltsine, Vladimir Poutine, Mikhaïl Gorbatchev, and Vladimir Lénine. I picked "c" but questioned the unusual spellings. You can't make up how you spell people's names! The list should have read: Boris Yeltsin, Vladimir Putin, Mikhaïl Gorbachev, and Vladimir Lenin. Those silly French.

But when I pondered it further (as you have plenty of time to do in the hospital) I realized the French are no more wrong than the Americans. These political leaders' names were originally written in the Cyrillic alphabet, so any attempt to convert to the Roman alphabet will mean you are simply making up the spelling. Who's to say the English spelling is any better than the French?

"Who was Luke's father in Star Wars?"

I'd forgotten how easy this show was. Anyone with half a brain would know the answer was Darth Vader.

Or "Dark Vador" as they translated into French. Now this one I had to disagree with. "Dark" is totally different from "Darth." And while I know the spelling change from "e" to "o" is to assist Francophones with pronunciation (lest they say "Dark Vad-*air*") I think the ruler of the Death Star would be mighty ticked off to see his name spelled wrong.

They don't stop there, either. R2-D2 is bizarrely called D2-R2, but only in Episode IV. Even when they correctly name him R2-D2, the pronunciation is incomprehensible. The first time I heard my husband say it, I thought he was having a stroke. "Err-duh-day-duh."

"What in the heck are you talking about?"

"You know, the guy in Star Wars that looks like a vacuum cleaner?"

"You mean R2-D2?"

"Same thing."

Tell that to George Lucas.

But our little Shop-Vac isn't the only robot to suffer a name change: C-3PO is Z-6PO. I can at least understand this one (it's because when dubbing into French, the way the actors' lips move when saying C-3PO is closer to Z-6PO in French) but I don't have to like it.

I flipped off the TV and decided to go to bed. Way too much brain activity for someone who was supposed to be resting. One quick visit to the bathroom and I'd be on my way to la-la-land.

Except greeting me in the bathroom was a humongous spider. No way could I sleep with that monster in the same room as me, but no way could I dispose of it either. It clung high on the wall and would require me to stand on a chair to swat at it. Pretty much the opposite of lying in a bed and taking it easy.

But what was I supposed to do? Page the nurse and ask her to kill a spider for me? That seemed silly.

"Mika, I need help," I said down the phone line.

"Oh my god, what is it? Are you OK?"

Whoops, I probably should have thought about my phrasing before sending my husband into a panic.

"I'm fine. Sorry. But there's a spider in my bathroom."

I didn't have to explain any further. He knew my fear of spiders and if anyone wanted me to take it easy more than me, it was my loving husband.

"Ask a nurse. They want their hospital to be clean and sterile. They won't mind."

"They won't think I'm silly?"

"Not at all."

"Should I press the button or wait for a nurse to come on her own? It doesn't seem to warrant pressing the call button."

"Doesn't someone come around for one last check before bed? Maybe you can wait until then?"

That sounded like the best plan. I crossed my fingers that the spider would stay put until then.

Fortunately, about five minutes later a nurse came in.

"Good evening, Madame. And how are we doing?"

"I'm good but I have a tiny problem."

Her face immediately took on a look of concern.

"There's a spider in my bathroom."

She laughed. "That's a problem we can fix. I'll be right back." I heard some smacking and a few "Oh la la's" before she returned with a smile on her face. "All done. Now let's take your temperature and blood pressure so you can go to sleep."

෧෬

Sunday morning I was all set to check out of my hotel. Catherine and Gilbert were babysitting Leo and Mika was cuddling with me in my hospital bed.

"As soon as I'm home, I need to send a few work emails to transition my projects," I said.

The doctors and *sage-femmes* would only release me if I promised to stay either on the couch or in bed all day, and I had an official document placing me on medical leave until the baby was born.

I thought of all the work I had left unfinished. I'd spent my last day in the office in one tiring meeting after another and hadn't had time to type up my notes and create action items for my team.

"I need to finish three spec docs, email status updates... Uh oh."

I felt a contraction as my belly hardened and started to bulge.

"What?" Mika asked.

"Nothing. Where was I? Yes, so I need to transition those projects plus create a task list for the U.S. website launch." I blabbed on as the contraction subsided, but another one came two minutes later.

"Are you having contractions?" he asked. "You have to tell me when that happens."

"I know, I just wanted to wrap up what I was saying."

"Vicki! This is serious. No more talking about work. You've been fine all weekend and haven't had a single contraction since they took you off the medicine, and the minute you talk about work they start up again. Coincidence?"

He was right. I promised to stop worrying about work.

Shortly after, a group of *sage-femmes* and doctors entered the room. "We can release you, as long as you haven't had any contractions."

I looked at Mika but before I could stop him, he tattled on me. "She just had a few contractions. Interestingly, while she was talking about work."

"Madame, you are officially off work until this baby comes. No talking about it, not even thinking about it, unless you want this baby to be born right now. We're going to have to keep you at least another day because of this, do you understand?"

Message received, loud and clear. The workaholic in me had to go if I wanted to keep this baby in.

30

Got Papers?

I CONTENTED MYSELF with reading and watching TV for the next 24 hours until I was released from the hospital. The seriousness of the situation had finally sunk in. This wasn't a one-time fluke, this was an ongoing threat that needed to be addressed. Mama was going to have to take it easy for up to fourteen more weeks. Yowza.

While I'd enjoyed my stay at the hospital—round-the-clock care, long restful nights, tasty meals served with a note wishing me "bon appétit"—it felt good to be home. The best part was being able to see my boys.

However, Leo was a bit confused.

He knew Mommy had gone away for a few days, not only because I wasn't there but because the house was an absolute *bordel*. Mika had done his best, but between worrying about his wife and unborn baby and caring for his son, household chores had fallen by the wayside.

Since I'd returned home, I'd been glued to one spot and had to wear compression stockings to avoid blood clots from lack of movement.

Leo approached me tentatively and eyed my stockings with suspicion. He pinched them. He pulled them. He couldn't figure out the correlation between the stockings and his new immobile Mommy but he knew there had to be one.

Then he spotted my belly, which seemed to have grown exponentially in the past four days. He rubbed it, poked my protruding belly button, then rested his head next to it.

All the better to keep his eye on it.

Within a few days, we fell into a new routine. Leo seemed less wary of the changes. Mika kept the house under control. I kept my booty on the couch.

"Great news!" Mika said, opening the mail one evening. "Leo's allergy test at the hospital has finally been scheduled."

When we first introduced Leo to formula at around four months, in preparation for going to the *crèche*, he'd had a severe allergic reaction. His skin erupted in hives in a matter of minutes and we had to rush him to the emergency room. They declared an allergy to cow's milk and we'd been avoiding it ever since.

We bought prescription formula for a small fortune but at least were partially reimbursed by *Sécurité Sociale*. I've had bottles of champagne that were less expensive, but that's more a testament to my undiscerning palate than the cost of the formula.

When Leo was old enough to try solids, we were amazed by how many prepackaged foods contained milk[13].

---

[13] Many people "helpfully" suggested we make our own baby food. Sure! I have loads of time! And my food processor is AWESOME. It

Why do mashed peas need milk? And nearly every cookie, cake, and other baby snack contained the off-limits ingredient.

Also, due to his allergy, we were advised by a specialist to steer clear of beef, fish, and eggs until he was one year old, then we could slowly introduce them one by one. Until then, it was Boring City in the food department. Purée, purée, and more purée. As a result, Leo celebrated his first birthday and still hadn't learned how to chew.

Day by day, we introduced new foods until he eventually got the hang of chewing. Before we knew it, he was gnawing on entire baguettes. So French! I was tempted to toss a beret on his mop of wavy dark hair and snap a photo. I would have if I owned a baby beret.

"That's wonderful!" I said. Leo's milk allergy testing was the last item to cross off the list before he'd have free rein of the food world.

Leo's blood results from five months prior showed that he'd outgrown his allergy. But that wasn't ample proof for the *crèche*—part of the French administration, remember—that he was now authorized to eat dairy. They had a royal decree (or at least they held it with the same reverence) that declared Leo allergic to cow's milk and nothing other than a new declaration from the hospital clearing him would allow him to consume cow's milk products at the *crèche*.

We'd tested a few organic cookies containing milk at home and Leo had no reaction. Well, no allergic reaction. He loved the flavor and went nuts over his new treat. I tasted one to see what the fuss was about and nearly tossed it across the room. Barf. I'll take Chips Ahoy over healthy organic crap any day. My hips are proof.

---

only splatters purée in every crevice of my kitchen, requiring 45 minutes of clean-up each time. And food processors are so cheap in Paris, you can buy them anywhere for the low price of €500. Making my own baby food is so fun and easy! I should do it for a living! Yeah, so we stuck to packaged foods. But at least we recycled the containers.

"It's maddening that they won't let him have cookies at the *crèche*," Mika had said after our successful cookie trial.

"I know, but the French gotta have their paperwork."

"I'm going to hide a box of cookies behind the toilet for him, Godfather-style."

I laughed. "Just don't get us kicked out of the *crèche* for smuggling illegal contraband."

Leo's test went off without a hitch. He was a ham, as usual, and the doctors and nurses fawned over him. He was having the time of his life, drinking milk and eating yogurt. It's cute how exciting things can be to someone who has never experienced them before. Milk! Yogurt! A whole universe to discover!

I was happy my son was able to get out there and enjoy life. I'd been stuck on the sofa for two weeks and could be there for up to twelve more. It was a weird feeling. I wanted Baby #2 to stay put as long as possible so she had the best chance of being born healthy. But each day she stayed in meant another day of me staying on the couch.

It would be rough, but totally worth it.

31

Sugar Waterita

"I miss you so much, Ammo!"

I'd met Anne Marie working at a bar the first week I arrived in Paris, close to a decade prior. After a few years, she switched jobs and started working at a new bar. It had been a huge shock for me—regulars do NOT like to change drinking establishments.

But then Ammo had really thrown me for a loop. She had moved to London the previous year, after falling in love and following a new career path. I was happy for her but missed her terribly. Who would I go out and cause trouble with?

"You stay home all the time anyway," she pointed out. "But yeah, I miss you, too. So how's it going with that baby?"

"My ass is growing larger by the day. I'm sure that would have happened anyway, but it doesn't help that I'm stuck on the couch."

"How much do you weigh now?"

Typical Anne Marie question.

"I'm not telling you!"

"I've never understood why people are so secretive about their weight. I can *see* you, you know. It's not like you're hiding anything." Good point.

"Well, I'm a pound or two over the recommended weight for this stage of my pregnancy, but I did just come back from a two-week trip to the U.S."

"Wasn't that in January?"

She really needed to stop being right.

"Yeah, but it's not like you can go on a diet when you're pregnant, so I'm stuck with it. That's not even the worst part, though. Mika keeps *losing* weight, I suppose from stress. If I'm not careful, I'll soon weigh the same as my 6'4" husband."

His sexy low-slung jeans were slung even lower these days, and his belt worked overtime just to hold them up.

"Don't worry about it. I'm only taking the piss. I'm sure you're fine. You don't want to be like those skinny French pregnant ladies. You see them from behind and don't even know they're pregnant."

"Trust me, you can tell from behind that I'm pregnant."

❧

Routine procedure during the second trimester of pregnancy is to have a gestational diabetes test. You have your blood drawn and provide a urine sample as a baseline. Then you drink pure sugar water and do the blood and urine samples again after an hour, then one last time after another hour.

While it's routine, they are particularly concerned in cases where the mom has gained excess weight. Like me. Throughout my pregnancy with Leo, my weight was only slightly higher than recommended, but every *sage-femme*, doctor, and busybody asked if I had gestational diabetes. And when my whopper of a preemie was born, no one believed my tests were negative.

No diabetes over here, guys. Just a tub of lard eating a tub of ice cream. It's amazing I only gained a few pounds.

As I was on strict bed rest with this pregnancy, I was only allowed out of the house for medical appointments. The blood test was the highlight of my month. I was going out on the town and drinking! Sure, I was drinking sugar water but I'd take it.

Mika accompanied me to the lab so he could check me in while I sat in the waiting room. I should have been able to reserve a spot in line while sitting in a chair, but you just know some French douchebag is going to steal your place in line if you don't actually stand there. Rather than risk our baby falling out at the blood lab, Mika braved the line for me.

"Here's your ID and insurance cards back," Mika said after signing me in. "Get this."

"What?"

"The entire test is covered by *Sécurité Sociale* except for the sugar. You have to pay €1 for that."

"Ha! No way. I wonder why? Maybe it counts as food and they don't cover food expenses?"

Though in my case it wasn't a meal, it was a party! Drinking a flavored concoction through a twisty straw was a downright blast these days. If the nurse could squeeze a lime in the bottle and run a little salt along the rim, I'd have a Sugar Waterita.

And if Anne Marie could hop over from London, we could have a proper party.

❧

The French healthcare system really is as good as its reputation. I received quality care that cost me next to nothing.

Which was fair because I'd followed every rule since immigrating to this country and paid a boatload of taxes.

Between Leo's stay in the NICU and my medical leave while on bed rest (which was 100% covered), I figure I got most of my money back. In fact, our supplemental health insurance—a primo package we signed up for through Mika's work—was so good that I actually got paid to have Leo.

Seriously.

Our hospital bills were lower than the amount allocated and so I received a check in the mail a few weeks after his birth. I won't tell you the amount or you'll be green with envy but it rhymes with schmeven schmundred euros.

Almost makes you want to have another baby. Almost.

32

The Terrible, Horrible, No Good, Very Bad Day

MY SIX-MONTH CHECK-UP at the hospital was straight out of hell. It had been three weeks since I'd gone into preterm labor and been prescribed strict bed rest. Other than for medical appointments, like my gestational diabetes party and a rockin' ultrasound, I hadn't left the house.

As a result, I became a bit of a hermit. I was apprehensive about the journey to the hospital for my next check-up.

Mika had ordered me a taxi, and the driver did me the favor of showing up 10 minutes early so that he could run up the meter. Luckily I saw that sneaky devil out of our apartment's front window, so I waddled down the stairs and got in the taxi early. Busted, bastard!

The meter was already at €9.20. Gee, thanks.

I asked the taxi driver to drop me off at the Emergency Room in order to avoid walking up the hill and stairs at the regular entrance. But he didn't know that was the reason—for all he knew I was already in labor.

The meter stopped at €11.80. I handed him €20 and asked for €8 back. One benefit of being practically French now is I don't have to tip like an American. Gone are the days of €3 tips for a four-minute ride. €0.20 would do just fine, and in this guy's case, was still way more than he deserved.

"What's with you people?" he shouted, snatching the 20-euro note with disgust. "Everyone expects me to make change. I'm not a bank! Why don't you go to the bank for change? You just expect *me* to make change! It's ridiculous."

Um… what? I hadn't asked him to break my twenty, I had asked for change back on a service provided. Completely different. It's not like I flagged down a taxi, requested change, and then went off to do laundry or toss a coin in a fountain.

And paying a €12 fee with €20 is not ridiculous. Unless I had a ten and a five or exact change, there's not a more efficient way to get the job done.

But more importantly, why was he yelling at a pregnant lady he was dropping off at the ER? Who does that?

"I'm sorry, sir, but I haven't been allowed to leave the house for three weeks." I tried to lighten the mood with a laugh, although in my fragile emotional state, I was trembling from the verbal attack. "I'm lucky I even have €20!"

He grunted and threw me my change. Then, bizarrely, he opened my door for me. I kept it together until I made it inside the hospital, then burst into tears. Fabulous.

Wiping the tears from my eyes, I trudged down the hall for the urine test. Then I waddled to the waiting room and lowered myself onto a padded folding chair. All set, with two minutes to spare.

Technically, I wasn't even supposed to sit for long

periods of time—I really should have been laying down—but a mysterious brown stain was splashed across the two empty chairs next to me. It was probably just coffee (didn't people see the "No Drinking, No Eating, Stay Skinny" sign?) but I didn't want to get any closer to find out.

Plus, the French ladies in the waiting room were perched daintily in their chairs, reading Vogue or Elle. I didn't want to sprawl out as if it were my living room.

I know I shouldn't have been so self-conscious and germaphobic, and I should have put my baby's safety ahead of myself. But as each minute ticked by I thought, "Surely the *sage-femme* will call me soon so it would be pointless to lie down now."

After twenty slow minutes had passed, when I was about to pass out from the infernal heat in the waiting room, a *sage-femme* I'd never seen before entered. "Madame Lesage?" she shouted in my general direction. Like the rest of her colleagues, she was impossibly pretty. Her dark curls fell loosely around her face, framing her gorgeous olive skin. But her bitchy attitude was apparent in her expression.

"Oui, that's me," I replied.

"I can't find your dossier." And then she just stood there with a pissed-off look on her face.

What did she want me to do about it? The hospital was responsible for the paperwork, not me. But since she seemed to expect an answer, I offered an explanation. "I was transferred to Port Royal when I went into preterm labor so maybe they still have my dossier?"

"That's impossible. Dossiers never leave the hospital."

It *was* possible. My dossier *did* leave the hospital. I know because it had been nestled next to me in my body bag on the gurney. But I didn't get the chance to say any of this because she clucked—literally clucked—and stormed off.

What had I done wrong? Was I supposed to work the

night-shift straightening their files? I couldn't help it if they were disorganized.

After ten long, uncomfortable minutes she returned and spat out, "They couldn't find it but I have another place to check. Wait here." Then she dashed off.

No need to worry, I wasn't going anywhere. I was queasy and surely green in the face, a fact she had missed in her haste to find my all-important file. What kind of a medical professional does that? Since when are papers more important than people?

I suspected I had another long wait ahead of me, so I caved in and lay down on the damn chairs. I knew I looked uncouth but I had to care more about the well-being of my baby than what the chic Parisian ladies in the waiting room thought. Preterm labor was still a serious risk and I couldn't take any chances, even with something as seemingly innocuous as sitting upright.

After another 15 minutes, Bitchface returned and led me to her office. "We have a student joining us today as well," she informed me.

Great. The more the merrier. I set my stuff down and immediately felt like I was going to faint. My vision started going black around the edges.

"We still don't have your dossier," she said in an accusatory tone.

And I still didn't understand why she was so mad at *me* about it. But I didn't have time to care. I needed to lie down, stat, or I would pass out.

I thrust my personal dossier into her hands. "The most recent papers, including the summary of my stay at Port Royal, are on top," I managed to get out. "I don't feel well. I need to lie down."

Then, to her horror, I lay down on the exam table before she had given me permission. Because, you know, when a patient is woozy and has already been waiting for nearly an hour when she's supposed to be on bed rest, the important thing is that she ask permission. We must observe niceties even if the room is spinning.

"Madame, you are not allowed to talk to me like that."

Huh? Talk like what? I'd relayed the information nicely and then lay down without asking first. I'd end up on the table at some point, better to do it before I fainted.

"I'm sorry but, as I said, I'm not feeling well. I'm supposed to be on bed rest so I need to lie down." With each word, I became more enraged. I shouldn't have to explain myself to her! I started to lose my cool. "Which I wasn't able to do while I was in the f-ing waiting room for 45 minutes."

I admit it's not polite to drop the f-bomb but the situation warranted it. It *was* an f-ing waiting room and I wanted her to know it.

"Whoa, whoa, whoa, Madame!" Bitchface shouted. "You are NOT allowed to talk to me like that. I will NOT be treated like that."

I backpedaled, scared of the screaming lady. "I'm sorry. Since I'm not French, sometimes I don't use the right words." That was a lie—I totally knew what *putain* meant but I needed to calm her down. Because, you know, as the distressed patient, *my* job was to calm *her* down.

"THAT'S NO EXCUSE! I'M A MEDICAL PROFESSIONAL AND I'M HERE TO HELP! YOU NEED TO RESPECT ME! I WILL NOT TREAT YOU UNTIL YOU STOP TALKING TO ME LIKE THAT."

"Then I will just stop talking." I felt the tears coming.

"I'M SERIOUS! YOU NEED TO CALM DOWN, MADAME. CALM DOWN! CALM DOWN! CALM DOWN!"

Was she talking to herself? Because *she* was the one who needed to calm down. Any minute now her head was going to spin around and spit pea soup.

At this point I was curled up in a ball on the exam table, crying my eyes out. Then—yay!—I had a contraction.

"I'm having a contraction," I whispered.

"Then you should relax."

"It would be easier if you stopped yelling at me."

"I'M NOT YELLING!"

I had my back to her and decided to keep my mouth shut for the rest of the appointment, instead drowning myself in uncontrollable tears. Two silent minutes passed, with my shuddering sobs being the only noises to break the stillness.

This was the exact opposite of what I needed to be doing to keep my baby in for another three months.

Finally, after shuffling through the dossier I had wisely brought, she walked over to the exam table. She pumped hand sanitizer on her palms and slowly massaged it into her skin. She gingerly approached me and placed a hand on my arm.

"Bonjour, I'm Sage-Femme Bitchface. I'd like to start us off on the right foot. Can we do that?"

I wanted to say "I f-ing hope so" but held my tongue. "OK," I said instead.

She walked on eggshells during the remainder of the appointment. I used the most polite tone I could muster.

We survived.

And the good news was that my condition was stable compared to my last check-up.

"Everything looks good, but you are still at risk of preterm labor occurring again. You must stay relaxed."

That would be easy, considering I didn't have to see that bitch until the following month.

33

¿Dónde Está El Baño?

IN MY JUNIOR HIGH FRENCH CLASS, I was Monsieur Assouad's teacher's pet. No surprise there, as I was pretty much every teacher's pet. While immature students were calling him Monsieur Asswad behind his back (which is admittedly funny, though not descriptive of his sweet personality), I was busy grading my fellow students' papers and placing orders for croissants at the nearby French café for French Pastry Day.

A native French-speaker himself, Monsieur Assouad focused on vocabulary and pronunciation. We were able to engage in petite conversations but our primary skill was to say random phrases perfectly. He knew better than to focus too much on grammar or he'd risk losing the class's already-waning attention.

And of course, we learned how to ask where the bathroom was. My friends who were taking Spanish or German learned the same phrase. We were all equipped to use the toilet if we ever headed overseas.

In high school we delved further into the French language. We learned how to ask where the bathroom was while practicing our grammar.

"Where is the bathroom?"

"Where was the bathroom?"

"Where will the bathroom be?"

If we ever went to a construction site in Paris, we could carry on quite the conversation with the work crew.

In college we learned verb tenses that I'm not even sure exist in English. "Imperfect" sounds like an insult rather than something we should spend months studying. "Pluperfect" sounds better—it literally translates to "more than perfect"—but I have no clue how to use that one either.

Even after six years of straight A's in French class, I indicated verb tense by adding "yesterday," "today," or "tomorrow" to my sentence, resulting in poetic beauties like "I eat sandwich yesterday, I eat pizza today, I eat onion soup tomorrow." Me Tarzan, you Jane.

By my ninth year living in France, I'd acquired a decent usage of the language. Enough to feel confident ordering in restaurants and leading company-wide presentations, but not enough to escape without numerous mistakes.

My 18-month-old son was uttering his first words, commencing with the typical "mama" and "papa," which worked in both French and English. Since bilingual children tend to start talking later, it bought me that much more time to improve my linguistic capabilities.

But he'd catch up before I knew it.

∾∾

"I can speak seven languages," my brother proclaimed at the ripe old age of four.

The bright Los Angeles sun reflected off Stephen's near-white hair. My six-year-old mind was both impressed by and doubtful of his statement.

"Prove it," I challenged. I wasn't letting him off that easy.

"OK, fine." He counted them on his fingers: "G'day mate. That's Australian. Sayonara… Japanese. Adios… Spanish. Bonjour… French. Top o' the morning! Irish. Aloha… Hawaiian. And of course English."

He held out seven fingers and beamed a triumphant smile at me.

I was baffled. Something told me he wasn't entirely right, but I couldn't be sure. One thing I did know was that I didn't like my younger brother speaking more languages than me. How had I let that happen?

We'd been living in California for about two years at that point. My mom called me a valley girl because I talked fast and sounded just like my mall-loving teenage counterparts. I was learning Spanish and sign language in school. I had a Japanese friend whose parents only spoke Japanese at home. I thought I was pretty cool.

If anyone should be rapidly firing off multiple languages, it was me.

❧

If my brother could "speak" seven languages at age four, I only had a little time left before my own child would surpass my current level of French.

Then again, I reminded myself, it wasn't a competition. My role was to teach him English and in fact, it would be better if I didn't even try to speak French to him. He heard French everywhere else—from Mika, Catherine and Gilbert, the *crèche*, the douchebags who frequently shouted in the street—and needed someone with a charming Midwestern American accent to teach him his second language.

So what if his French was better than mine? That could

only be a good thing.

Week by week, Leo's language skills exploded. Rather than wasting energy on nouns (hello, he had ten fingers he could point with in order to accomplish that), he picked up incredibly cute phrases:

Bravo!

Often accompanied by a round of his own applause, usually after he'd done something he thought was amazing, like standing on the table and dancing. I wonder where he got that from? Throw a glass of wine in his hand and he'd be the spitting image of Mama.

Ah, non!

Said with an authentic French nasal accent, this one came out whenever something dramatic happened, like spotting a mess on the other side of the room. Again, I wonder where he got that from?

Oh la la!

Less severe than "ah, non!" he used this for casual mishaps, like dropping his croissant. I always thought this phrase was a cliché, but French people really do say it.

Non, pas ça!

Much stronger than a simple "no," he used this to express "no, not that!!!" in such dire situations as needing to have his diaper changed or after we'd turned off his music.

Au revoir!

After all my years of schooling and living in France, I still can't say this right. I've adapted by saying "Ciao," playing off of my Italian heritage and acting like I'm too cool for the banal "Au revoir." And yet my son had perfected it, even throwing in a wave of his hand.

I was sure his next phrase would be "Where is the bathroom," particularly since we were about to start potty training him.

That question was easy to answer—just look for Mommy because at seven months pregnant, it's where she was spending most of her time.

34

I Spy with My Little Eye

"BONJOUR, MADAME LESAGE?"

A woman with a sweet voice and a blocked number had called my cell phone. I was wary of answering in case I had to deal with rapid-fire French, but in the end my curiosity won out and I'd answered.

"Oui, c'est moi," I responded cautiously.

"Yes, my name is Adrienne and I'm a *sage-femme libérale*. I will do your check-up next week instead of Véronique. How does Monday morning sound?"

Ever since my hospital release, Véronique, a bubbly *sage-femme* with close-cropped salt-and-pepper hair, had been checking in on me once per week.

French health care at its finest.

She was patient, friendly, and thorough. She assuaged my fears about every kick and twinge and reminded me to "Keep Calm and Stay on the Couch."

Each week she arrived with her travel-sized kit containing a stethoscope, blood pressure cuff, urine test strips, and even a portable baby heart rate monitor.

How cool was that?

However, Véronique had informed me at the last visit that she would be on vacation for the next two weeks (French vacation system at its finest) and that another *sage-femme* would do the check-up. Coupled with my recent horrible hospital appointment, I was scared to let a new *sage-femme* into my home.

"Um, sure, that's fine."

"Madame, are you alright? You can tell me." Adrienne's tone was so gentle that the dam burst and I let everything loose.

"Now that you ask, no, I'm not alright. The *sage-femme* at my last appointment was the meanest lady on the planet and she made me cry and she didn't even answer any of my questions and now I'm stressed and worried and upset."

"I'm sorry to hear that, Madame. On behalf of L'Hôpital Trousseau I apologize. Let me check your dossier real quick," she said, as I heard her flip several pages. "Ah, Sage-Femme Bitchface. Yes, I know her. This isn't the first time I've heard she can be, um, harried during her appointments."

"That's one way to put it." Though I knew she couldn't put it any other way. Calling your colleague an evil bitch, no matter how well-deserved, isn't professional.

"How about I come Monday morning and I promise to stay as long as necessary to answer your questions."

"Thank you, that sounds fantastic."

Thank God they weren't all miserable cows.

House calls were fabulous, particularly since my only outing in the past month had been horrendous. But it was still hard to stay on the sofa. Weeks ticked by and while that meant great news for the development and health of my baby, it also meant that Mama was slowly going crazy.

It helped having floor-to-ceiling French windows (or simply "windows" as they're called here) on the side of our apartment facing the road. Our narrow two-lane street was actually a main thoroughfare in the neighborhood and saw a lot of traffic—both pedestrian and automobile. I observed fascinating scenes out that window from the comfort of my perch:

My father-in-law walking home from work.

To avoid boredom after working at the same company for 30+ years, Gilbert alternates between four different evening commuter routes. One of them passes in front of our house. It amazes me how often I've spotted him, considering I would have to look up within the exact five seconds he happens to be walking in front of our window. Sometimes in a city this big, you forget how small the world can be.

People being idiots at the gate.

A metal fence with scary spikes protruding from the top separates the street ruffians from the tenants of our building. Not that there's much riff-raff in this part of town, but the benches in our courtyard park could be quite enticing for homeless people and drunks. Sorry, but I pay way too much rent to allow that to happen.

To open the gate, you can either enter the four-digit code on the keypad or swipe your key fob. The gate takes 1.2 seconds to open, which is 1.1 seconds longer than people are willing to wait. So they swipe their fob multiple times or bang on the digicode keypad, cursing the door and demanding that it open. This in turn confuses the gate, which often ends up getting stuck in the one-inch open position.

"C'est quoi cette merde?" What is this crap, they'll shout.

I want to shout back, "*You're* the piece of *merde* who

pushed the button too many times!'"

To address the problem, the concierge installed a snazzy engraved sign instructing "Please wait one second, you impatient jerks, before trying the gate again." Not that anyone reads the sign.

The most frustrating scene to watch is when this blind man in our building comes or goes. He always follows the correct procedure, swiping his fob and waiting for the gate to open. The mechanism is nearly silent so I don't know if he listens for it to open or just has the rare (for a resident of our building) ability to wait one second. Then he walks forward.

But inevitably some impatient moron on the other side will have pressed the button in the meantime and sent the gate on the fritz, causing Nice Blind Guy to walk right into it.

Seriously, people. It's one second! Can't you wait?

People leaving the hospital with their babies.

Across the street is L'Hôpital Diaconnesses, which specializes in delivering babies. It's a great hospital for moms and newborns who don't have any complications. It's run by nuns, many of whom live in our building, making it the second time this Catholic schoolgirl has lived near nuns since moving to Paris. Is the universe trying to send me a message?

When Leo was born at Trousseau, we noticed that many of the other babies in the NICU had been transferred from Diaconnesses after experiencing problems. That's a hassle we didn't need, so for Baby #2 we thought it best to stick with what we knew and register at Trousseau from the start, despite missing out on the convenience of Diaconnesses being within spitting distance.

Our building faces the hospital's exit, so I witness a steady stream of new parents walking out, half-proud/half-scared expressions on their faces. The husband is usually carrying the baby in a car seat while the mom holds her husband's arm and smiles as she hobbles next to him, trying to ignore the throbbing pain of her episiotomy scar.

They arrive at their car and attempt to install the car seat.

It starts out civil, with mom standing politely off to the side as dad fools around with the seatbelt and the car seat.

"Why don't you try looping it under the thingimijig," mom will suggest.

"I already looped it twice around the thingimijig," dad will reply, an edge to his voice.

"I'm only trying to help."

"I don't need any help. I just need this piece of *merde* to snap in place!"

"Maybe you should have practiced before the baby was born."

That's what *I'm* saying, mama!

"Maybe I didn't have time with all the other crap you've been asking me to do."

"You sure had enough time to watch football. Now I'm standing here with my lady bits hurting to high hell and having a hot flash and you still haven't figured out the damn seatbelt."

"If you'd stop nagging me, woman, I could get the job done!"

"I hardly think the nagging is why you're so inept at this."

"Did you forget to take your pain pills today?"

"Did you forget to turn on your brain today?"

Time to pop some popcorn and watch the show. I'd want to shout something helpful, but then they'd know I'd been spying.

But, hello, every baby book tells you to practice installing the car seat before you go to the hospital. And I can't tell you how many times the parents would put the car seat facing forward instead of backward. I would toss piece after piece of buttery goodness into my mouth, watching with bated breath until they realized they needed to turn the darn thing around.

"Oh, *there's* the thingimijig the seatbelt is supposed to go through," dad would say.

"I told you."

"You did not."

"Let's just go before our baby goes off to college."

People engaging in suspicious behavior.

One pleasant night during my pregnancy, I woke up with a massive case of acid reflux. The kind so bad I'd been dreaming about going to the pharmacy to buy reflux medicine, which triggered my brain to wake me up. Yay.

I popped a reflux pill, then headed for my routine bathroom break. I blew my nose, resulting in a nosebleed. I'd also been suffering through a cold and started having an uncontrollable coughing fit.

The fun during pregnancy never ends.

I installed myself on the couch with a tissue held to my nose, sucking merrily on a cough drop, and had just booted up my computer when a movement at the hospital gates drew my eye.

A heavyset man skirted awkwardly along the edges of the driveway, burdened by the weight of a huge duffel bag. He dumped it in the outdoor stairwell, then hurried back to whatever dark corner he'd come from.

I checked the clock on my computer. 3:15 am.

That was odd. But it had probably been routine hospital procedure. I turned my attention to Facebook, planning to catch up on important updates like what my friends in the U.S. had for dinner that night.

Then another movement caught my attention. A white car pulled up in front of the gate and stopped right there in the street.

A tall, wiry man emerged from the vehicle, looked both

ways, then flicked a cigarette on the ground. He passed through the gate to the stairwell, snatched the duffel bag, returned to the car, and glanced around him once more before hefting the cargo into the trunk.

He dashed to the front seat, then sped away.

Had I witnessed a back alley deal? Surely any legit hospital activity would have happened during the day. And the men would be wearing uniforms, and the driver's car would have been marked with "Organ Transplant Vehicle" or something similar, right?

Or maybe not.

Considering postal workers and cashiers don't wear uniforms here (which always throws me off—like, are you sure you work here?) maybe organ transplant employees don't either. All I can say is if you're giving me someone's kidney, you should at least wear a name tag.

Unusual deliveries.

The residents of my building have all sorts of stuff delivered but it's rarely interesting. Groceries, flowers, furniture. Sometimes a huge piece of furniture shows up that you know isn't going to fit through any of the doorways or stairwells so you just sit back and watch the show.

But the weirdest delivery was one to the hospital. An unmarked truck pulled up and two burly guys exited the cab and headed around to the back of the vehicle.

What were they going to unload? So exciting!

Or not.

Turns out their wares were coffins[14]. And not modern-

---

[14] Get out your pen and paper, kids, because we're going to learn something today. The word "coffin" comes from the French word "cofin." "Cofin" originally meant "basket," but as the languages morphed over the years, it became "coffin" in English and "couffin" in French, which came to mean "cradle." That just sent shivers down my spine. And yet another fascinating fact: in North America we tend to

looking ones, either. The six-sided pine structures were each adorned with a metal cross, and I couldn't be sure but possibly cobwebs draped down the sides. I expected a vampire to jump out at any second.

What really gave me the heebie jeebies (apart from Dracula's bed being carried down the street) was that they were entering the maternity hospital. Why on earth would they need full-size creepy adult coffins there?

I called Mika to find out.

"That makes sense. In addition to being a maternity, Diaconnesses is also a geriatric hospital. They handle the beginning and the end."

That gave me a whole new bout of heebie jeebies.

"But why does a hospital need coffins? I know people can die in a hospital but don't they usually transfer the body to a funeral home?"

"I think this place has a funeral home in it. Or at least a morgue with a crematorium. I've seen it before."

The hairs on my arm stood on end. I focused on the pregnant ladies waddling out and the new parents proudly carrying their little cabbages. Much better than thinking about what happened on the other side.

Waving to my son.

My 19-month old son was turning out to be an attention hog like me. I couldn't wait to take Leo to his first karaoke bar.

Until then, we established an elaborate window-waving ritual, which was by far the best thing I saw out of my window. It wasn't as good as being able to drop him off and pick him up from daycare myself (or actually hold him or play with him), but it was our special moment.

---

use "coffin" to describe the six-sided funerary box (meaning, the long sides extend at an angle where the person's arms are crossed) and "casket" to refer to the rectangular version (where the long sides are straight).

We would blow kisses to each other and make a heart shape with our fingers. But Leo's favorite was my finger guns. I would hold my hands like guns and kiss the "barrel" of each one, then go "pew, pew, pew" as I shot bullet kisses at him. Passersby rightly gave me odd looks but I didn't care because my adorable son would always raise his finger guns and shoot me kisses back.

If I couldn't be a part of his life outside the house, I could at least shoot him.

Confessions on Bed Rest

I'D MADE IT THROUGH four weeks of bed rest and had anywhere from one day to ten weeks left. It sucked looking out the window and seeing the world passing me by. Soon it would be spring and I wanted so badly to join the ranks of Parisians soaking in sunshine and wine at a sidewalk café.

And I would love to not have to worry that my baby would fall out on the way to the bathroom.

But it wasn't all bad.

I wish I could pick up my son, I honestly do. But I don't mind letting Mika deal with his tantrums, wipe up the food splattered on the wall, wash the dishes, fold the laundry, and then do it all over again the next day. It's hard to be stuck on the sofa but sometimes it is the perfect cop-out.

We will never truly know what caused my preterm labor. But I find it interesting that it happened right after my hardest and most stressful day of work. It was amazing how quickly the workaholic in me evaporated and how easily I was able to adjust to spending my days in one spot instead of running from meeting to meeting.

The Internet helped (thank you, Al Gore!). It's astonishing the number of funny posts I would miss from George Takei's Facebook page if I had to work all day long.

You've gotta see the bright side in bed rest, right?

35

So What Cha Want?

"HERE'S THAT YOGURT I was talking about," Catherine said, handing me a grocery bag full of her new favorite treat.

Mika shot me a knowing glance. Many a time I had made fun of the French for eating yogurt as a dessert, and now here my mother-in-law had bought me a "special" kind. How could yogurt be special? It's yogurt. You'd be hard-pressed to find a more boring product on the planet. And this is coming from someone who doesn't bore easily, having once read an LSAT prep book for fun, with no intention of ever becoming a lawyer.

"Thanks, that's really nice of you. So, what makes this yogurt so special?"

"It's for *les grosses faims*," she said, beaming with pride as if she had invented this new concoction.

I knew that meant "big hungers" and assumed the yogurt was richer and creamier and probably loaded with extra calories. It might not be half-bad. But I couldn't let her off this easy.

"For *les grosses femmes*? I've been stuck on the sofa a long time but I'm not *that* fat!"

The French love a good play on words and this opportunity was ripe for the pickin' since "big hunger" sounds a lot like "fat lady" in French.

"Good one, Vicki," she said. "You know your French is good when you can make a joke."

I may be fat and I may eat yogurt for dessert, but at least I'm funny!

"So," she continued, "people have been asking me what you need for Baby #2. Have you created a registry?"

Catherine meant business. When Leo was born, we received a mountain of gifts. The Lesage family bombarded us with trendy outfits and practical gear and everything in between, but even Catherine's colleagues showered us with presents. And the mother of one of her coworkers knitted us an adorable baby blanket. While you don't traditionally receive as many gifts for a second baby, I knew that Catherine's circle of friends and family was a generous exception.

Luckily I'd already created an online list in anticipation of this. Good thing I had all day free on bed rest since it practically took that long.

In the U.S., you would probably go to Target or Babies R Us (or Pottery Barn Kids if you're trying to run your friends broke) and scan a bunch of stuff, finishing your registry in time for happy hour (with virgin daiquiris, of course). Or, since it's not the Stone Age, you might create one online in a matter of minutes.

Not in France.

They don't have a one-stop-shop like Target where you can register online. There are a few stores similar to Target but forget about a registry.

I opted to create our list at a baby clothing store that also sold a few other items, like bedding and furniture.

I set up an account and started browsing through clothes before I realized I couldn't select the size. Why not? Why wouldn't they make that option available? Given my experience with French sizes, I wanted to be able to specify that we needed larger sizes. If I couldn't indicate my selection, then what was the point of having a registry? I'd end up with 30 doll-sized dresses that my baby girl wouldn't have time to wear before she outgrew them.

Since I'd already opened a stupid account, I decided to browse their non-clothing selection for the few remaining items on my list. But guess what? You can't add them to the registry! Why not? Who the hell knows!

I abandoned the site and tried to forget the hour I'd wasted there.

I blew another hour browsing French baby sites but they either didn't offer registries or didn't have a wide enough selection to be worth my time. Was I going to have to create fifty separate registries?

That gave me an idea. Maybe I could piece together the items I wanted into one list? That's when I found MesEnvies.fr ("My Wishlist"). You copy and paste a link from anywhere on the internet and it generates an entry with a photo, description, and price of the item.

The fact that a site like this even exists is a testament to the failure of all the other French baby sites. I'm trying to give you my business (or, at least, my family's business)! Let me sign up for crap that my hormones are telling me I need and let nice people buy it for me! Why are you making this so hard, France?

Of course, even MesEnvies.fr is not without flaws. Their login system was built for the internet of 1994. You don't have a username, you just enter your first and last name. What happens when someone with the same name signs up? Maybe they didn't foresee that happening, figuring they'd only get a handful of sign-ups. Probably a good assumption, since most people would have given up hours before I did.

"Yep, Catherine, we have a list," I said. "I'll email you the link. Thanks for spreading the word."

Maybe my day's worth of work would go to some use after all.

36

Expiration Date

HAVING LIVED IN PARIS FOR NINE YEARS, I'd experienced my fair share of bureaucracy[15]. For my first five years in this gloriously bureaucratic nation, I freelanced for American companies, which necessitated renewing my long-stay tourist visa each year. Which itself necessitated mounds of paperwork including: birth certificate issued within the past six months (really? What would have changed since the one issued a year ago?), passport, a year's worth of bank statements, Warren Buffet-sized stashes of money that I couldn't touch, my own private health insurance, and a sworn oath not to murder any employees of the state.

Well, maybe not that last one but for their own sake, they should add it to the list.

---

[15] For some reason, every time I type that word it comes out "bureaucrazy." Spell-check fixes it for me, but should it? My subconscious may be on to something.

Then I got a job in a French office. While my company sponsored my work visa, I still had to handle the paperwork myself. Which was all of the above plus a bunch of certificates proving I'd taken my "Intro to French Absurdity" classes. I passed with flying colors, having witnessed plenty of madness during the previous five years.

After I got married, I tried to switch my visa status to one that was linked to my husband, rather than my job. The intention was to acquire a ten-year permanent resident card to save myself the annual hassle, but as I was missing an item that hadn't even been on the list (I'd forgotten to read their minds that day), it was denied. I was instead issued a one-year resident visa and told to renew it the next year, when I would be eligible to apply for the ten-year card.

"Honey, no," Jocelyne the Mean Government Worker had said during my yearly appointment at the Préfecture. "I don't know who said you could apply for the ten-year card, but you don't have enough proof of *vie commune* yet."

I was pretty sure *she* was the one who had provided this information at the last meeting but I'd long since learned to shut my trap, take notes on what I needed to provide, and come back later. Apparently she needed more proof that Mika and I were a true couple and that I wasn't just in it for the visa. You'd think the baby we brought with us would have helped prove our claim, but as he wasn't a piece of paper, he didn't count.

Finally, this year I was prepared to apply for my ten-year resident card. I had gathered all of the items on Jocelyne's list and then some. I made two copies of each document and donated money to a tree-planting charity in an effort to offset the horrifying amount of papers I'd had to print off.

The only problem now was the timing.

Jocelyne had instructed me at the previous meeting to schedule my 2014 appointment no earlier than three months in advance of my visa's expiration date (because the website couldn't schedule appointments sooner than that) and no later than two months in advance (because they would be booked up). Since my visa expired on February 12th, I made a note in my calendar to sign on to the website on November 12th.

On November 12th, the Préfecture's website greeted me with the news that everything was booked until April 11th. Bastards. A bright red message implored applicants to book four to five months before the expiration date of their visa.

Jocelyne was a lying liar who lied! Or at least grossly misinformed.

But what could I have done instead? Anticipated her incompetence and checked the website every day in case they changed their policy? I wouldn't have time to stuff my face with croissants if I did that.

With a sigh, I accepted the April 11th appointment.

"Mika, your country is driving me crazy," I said over dinner that night.

"What's it this time?" He was not the least bit surprised by my statement.

I filled him in and he offered to find a solution. I was worried about having an expired visa from February 12th to April 11th.

After weeks of emails and phone calls with the Préfecture, he received an answer. But shhh, I didn't tell you this.

Apparently, an expired visa is still valid as long as you have a *convocation* (official notice) for a future date. The convocation serves as an extension of your visa, but you must carry it with you at all times in case you get stopped by a police officer.

Why was I not surprised? The French had built in a backup plan because they knew loads of people would be walking around with expired visas. I'd be upset about their nonchalance toward the term "expired" except that it meant I was in legal compliance until April 11th.

Whew.

Except, as you might remember (I've only been blathering on about it for the past few chapters), I was prescribed strict bed rest on January 31st and was not allowed to leave the house, except for medical reasons, until my baby arrived.

Calculating a typical four-day hospital stay after giving birth, I'd have to have Baby #2 on April 7th (six weeks before my due date) in order to be available by April 11th.

"I'd hate to miss my appointment but I'd hate even more for my baby to be six weeks premature," I complained to Mika. "It was so tough going through that with Leo."

Ever the wonderful husband, he called the Préfecture to see what he could work out.

"No dice, babe. I called at lunch and they said you can't schedule a new appointment until you've missed the existing one."

"But we know we're going to miss this one! Or we're like 99% sure we are. Wouldn't it be better to reschedule now, especially considering it takes five months to get an appointment?"

"Preaching to the choir. It's dumb. But they said we have to wait until April 12th to reschedule."

"Well, they're really dumb because April 12th is a Saturday."

"Ha, figures. I'll call them on April 14th and sort it out."

"I hope I don't get busted over the weekend."

Though considering I'd be stuck inside, it was a pretty safe bet.

What a Sisyphean task. We'd wait until April 14th to reschedule, when I'd likely be given a date for September. As long as I had the *convocation*, I'd be in legal compliance, even though my visa would be seven months expired by then.

Here's where it got ridiculous (well, more ridiculous than it already was). When renewing a visa, they retain its original expiration date and simply update the year. If I succeeded in acquiring my ten-year resident card, it would expire on February 12, 2024. But if for some reason (any reason, like Jocelyne was in a pissy mood) my ten-year resident card didn't get approved and I was stuck with another one-year card, that card would expire on February 12, 2015.

Considering you had to book your renewal appointment five months in advance, that would mean the minute I walked out the door of the Préfecture, I'd have to hop online to schedule my next meeting.

French bureaucracy was killing me. Did I even want a ten-year card anymore? What would another decade with these people do to me?

37

Men in Uniform

"OH MY GOSH HE'S SO CUTE!"

Though I should have been on the couch, I had allowed myself two minutes to play with Leo while he took his bath. Papa couldn't have all the fun! And I just couldn't resist my pudgy toddler splish-splashing in the tub. It was his favorite time of the day (aside from slamming pots and pans together and listening to music on the iPad) and he was a joy to watch.

"I know," Mika said. "I just love this guy. I can't believe we're going to have another baby soon. They're both going to break the cute-o-meter!"

I shared Mika's sentiment. I mean, I could believe we were going to have another baby—my pregnant belly and continual presence on the sofa made it hard to forget—but at the same time, I couldn't clearly picture it. We'd been so focused on the pregnancy and preterm labor that sometimes we forgot about the actual baby that was about to enter our lives.

"Well, I've used up my standing time for the day. I'll meet you in the bedroom."

I headed into the room we shared with Leo (gotta love large Parisian apartments!) and lay on our bed to wait for the boys to finish bath time. I was breathless from the brief exertion. And my heart was racing. Man, I was out of shape. But I had no choice since exercise was expressly forbidden.

"Where's Leo? There he is!"

Mika stood at the bedroom door, holding our wet baby and playing peek-a-boo with his ducky bath towel. Leo cracked up, as if it was the funniest thing he'd ever seen, even though Mika did that every night.

"Bring that cutie pie over to me!" I called from the bed.

As Mika and Leo approached, I noticed my son's skin had a bluish hue. And his teeth were chattering.

"That's weird. Is he cold?"

Normally Leo sported as little clothing as he could get away with, tearing his pants off as soon as he ran through the front door. He was hot-blooded and I'd never seen him shiver before, except when exposed to the Siberian temperatures during our trip through Chicago.

"He doesn't feel cold," Mika said, laying him on the bed. "But listen. Do you hear that wheezing? Sounds like he's having trouble breathing."

"Crap. Let's take his temperature and get him dressed."

Mika took rectal thermometer duty while I dressed our baby. His temperature indicated a fever, yet his teeth were still chattering and his skin color hadn't returned to normal.

What the heck was going on?

I started to head back to the living room but Leo grabbed me, hugged me, and didn't let go. For a full minute. Sounds sweet but it had me worried. As much as my son loved me, he rarely cuddled for longer than a nanosecond. No time to waste when there were pots to bang!

I caught Mika's eye and saw he was thinking the same thing. Something was up.

"Let's do a test," I suggested. "Will you bring him over to his kitchenette and see if he plays?"

One of the hundred Christmas presents Catherine and Gilbert had spoiled Leo with was a miniature kitchen set from Ikea. Its neutral wood and simple design matched our apartment. Which was good since that's where we kept our dishes.

For the first few weeks after we had set up his new toy, we tried to keep Leo's pots in his kitchenette and our pans in the real kitchen. But inevitably he would wander into our kitchen, steal some supplies, and stock up his own kitchen. Rather than waste time looking between the two, Mika had simply moved everything out of our bottom cabinets and stored them in Leo's play set.

The kid could play for hours, dumping fake veggies from container to container, beating utensils against lids, and cooking his stuffed bunny for dinner (he is part French after all).

Mika set Leo in front of the kitchenette and we waited for his reaction. He picked up a spatula and tapped it half-heartedly against the plastic sink, then began wheezing.

He was definitely sick.

"I don't mean to be paranoid but–" I started.

"I'm calling emergency."

"Whew, yes," I said, relieved we were in agreement about the severity of the situation. "But maybe just tell them he's short of breath, not that he hugged his mom and isn't in the mood to cook. They might not have the same checklist for warning signs that we do."

The phone operator took us seriously and immediately dispatched a team of paramedics.

Within minutes, an ambulance pulled up in front of our building and out hopped three gorgeous *pompiers*, French paramedics/firemen. Maybe it was because I felt dizzy, but

I was pretty sure they were walking in slow motion, just like in the movies.

As if my heart hadn't been racing enough with the exertion of bath time and then worrying over my son's health, now these heartthrobs were on their way to my apartment. And I was a beached whale on the couch, dressed in my usual tank top, yoga pants, and compression stockings. Can we say sexy?

"Bonsoir," Mika said, opening the door to the *pompiers*, Leo in his arms.

"Bonsoir. Monsieur Lesage?"

"Oui."

"And we're here for Monsieur Leonardo Lesage?"

"Oui."

"OK, let's check him out."

They marched into the bedroom, each of the *pompiers* greeting me with a "Bonsoir, Madame" as they passed the living room.

Gorgeous *and* well-mannered? Good thing I already had an incredibly polite husband who was the handsomest in the land, otherwise I might have had to pour these *pompiers* a glass of wine and get to know them a little better.

I couldn't hear what was happening in the bedroom so Mika came back every few minutes with updates.

"They suspect he might have gone into mild shock due to the temperature difference in and out of the bath, especially since he's running a slight fever."

Two minutes later: "They're not too worried overall, except his breathing is still labored."

Four minutes later: "Leo's acting like he doesn't have a care in the world, which is good, but he's noticeably quieter than usual. Which means he's probably sick. The *pompiers* can't find anything wrong with him but I need to take him to the hospital. It's protocol for any child under two."

Now my heart was really racing. Mentally, I remained calm because it didn't sound that serious. But physically I was dizzy, short of breath, and could hear my heart pounding in my chest.

"Are you OK, honey?" Mika asked, noticing the beads of sweat forming on my forehead.

"Um, probably. But maybe one of the *pompiers* should have a look?"

Talk about a drama queen. The paramedics came for my son and now I was stealing the attention with a panic attack.

"Madame Lesage?"

A young *pompier* with a buzz cut, in his full fireman's uniform, walked into the living room.

"Your husband told me you're not feeling well."

"It's silly, I know, but I think I'm having a panic attack."

"OK, just lie down and I'll check you out."

In any other situation I'd ask him to at least buy me a drink first. But for once I kept my witty little mouth shut.

He checked my heart rate and blood pressure. Everything was normal.

"Try to relax, Madame Lesage," he said, packing up his equipment. "I know it's hard. Leaning back can be better than lying all the way down, so you might want to try that position."

It took all my willpower not to say "That's what she said." And yes, I know I have the humor of a teenage boy.

Mika came back to the living room holding Leo, who was wearing a diaper, a onesie, and slippers. "Everything OK, Mama?"

"I'm fine, I just need to chill out. So you're going to the hospital?"

"Yep, we're heading out with the *pompiers*. We get to ride in the ambulance."

"Leo is going to love that, aren't you sweetie?"

Leo smiled at me, still a bit dazed.

"I'll call you with updates, but try to take it easy," Mika

said, kissing me goodbye. "I love you."

"I love you, too. And I love *you*, cutie pie," I said, kissing Leo on the cheek.

"Bonne soirée, Madame Lesage," the *pompiers* said as they filed out the door.

Mika grabbed a blanket to wrap around our half-naked baby. I couldn't believe Leo was going out in public dressed like that but it was too late. I watched from the window as the five of them piled into the ambulance.

Leo was in heaven.

He'd watched ambulances pull in and out of the hospital before (clearly he gets his curiosity from his spy-happy mother) and now he had the chance to ride in one himself. He waved to me from the backseat, leaving me with a happy image to calm my nerves for the next who-knew-how-many hours.

Until they returned, I was stuck on the sofa by myself. Worrying about my boys at the hospital. Even with frequent reports from Mika I still had a hard time staying as zen as I knew I needed to be.

Once Baby #2 was born, the roles would be switched—Mika and Leo would be home at night while Mama and baby were at the hospital, for at least four days. I would tell Mika not to worry and he would worry anyway.

Do you ever reach a time, as a parent, when you're not constantly worrying about your children?

38

Stella!

APRIL 20, 2014 WAS A BIG DAY. Christians and chocolate bunny lovers around the world celebrated Easter. Pot smokers lit up to celebrate 420. George Takei celebrated his birthday.

And Mama was finally off bed rest.

I'd made it through eight months of pregnancy and was now free to unfasten my seatbelt and move about the cabin. Not that my big fat belly and atrophied muscles allowed me to go very far, but it was better than nothing.

I started slowly, with 10-minute walks around the neighborhood. On April 24, the birthday I wanted for my daughter, I allowed myself a longer walk and danced around the apartment with Leo.

But days ticked by and, despite having threatened to come months earlier, this baby wasn't budging. Looks like I'd been a little too good at lying on the couch!

"I guess she won't have an even numbered birth date," I said to Mika on May 1st. We were out of April, and with a due date of May 20th we now knew she would be born sometime in May. "But I'm not complaining. Every day she's in there is better for her."

I felt I didn't have the right to complain but man, those last few weeks of pregnancy were as brutal as everyone had warned. Every position I tried was uncomfortable, acid reflux burned my throat nonstop, and my lungs were so compressed I was constantly short of breath.

It hadn't been as bad with Leo since he came early, and while I would prefer discomfort to a preemie, it was hard to say I preferred discomfort when I was suffering through it.

"She could come any day now, but remember, she could come as late as the 20th," Mika said. "I know it's hard to wait that long. Maybe a foot rub would help?"

That definitely helped.

∽✌

A few more sleepless nights passed and I still acted like I was in no hurry for the baby to come, even though it was all I could think about.

To distract me, and to prepare Leo for the arrival of his sister, Mika bought our son a baby doll. We got the idea from the *crèche*, where the children care for their own baby dolls, even giving them a bath every morning!

Leo immediately knew what to do, though of course he wasn't gentle about it. He slammed the bottle into the baby's mouth, ripped its clothes off for bath time, and plopped the doll down on its miniature potty seat. Then he took his stuffed animals (*doudous* in French) and one by one lined them up on the toilet.

My own miniature potty trainer! Bossy and organized, just like his mama. He wasn't quite ready to use the toilet himself but he knew how to run the show for everyone else.

Hopefully he would display the same enthusiasm for his sister.

And maybe with a smidge more tenderness.

At 12:30 am on May 4th, two weeks after I'd been allowed off bed rest, I went into labor. I'm happy to report that the delivery went about as smoothly and uneventfully as possible. Which seemed fair after all I'd gone through the previous three months!

The taxi driver had been thrilled, the *sage-femmes* and nurses were excellent, and much as I expected a sensational addition to my story, I only found your typical birth experience.

Until I checked into my hotel room (yep, still called it that). As the orderly wheeled me down the hall, my legs still numb from the epidural, who did I see at the nurse's station?

Sage-Femme Bitchface.

We made eye contact. She looked at me as if she hadn't been a total cow several months earlier. I looked at her as if I hadn't written an entire chapter about her.

"Bonjour," she said.

"Bonjour!" I chirped back.

Go figure. I'd lucked out and hadn't had any additional monthly check-ups with her, and thank God she hadn't been the one to deliver my baby. But she just had to show up in my final days at the hospital.

"Is that…?" Mika whispered.

"Yep," I replied. Clearly my description of the devil incarnate had been accurate if he could recognize her from a simple bonjour.

"Well, no one can bring my mood down," he said, patting the sleeping baby in my arms. "I have a beautiful baby girl!"

"I know!"

I gazed down at Stella[16] Catherine Lesage. My pregnancy had seemed to last years. It had been full of concern for my baby girl's health and fear of an early arrival, and now here she was. I couldn't have been happier.

§◊§

"Where's Leo?" I called from my hospital bed as I heard my son and husband approach down the corridor. I hoped neither of them was contemplating a career as a spy, considering they sounded like a troop of baboons.

Leo peeked his head around the door.

"There he is!" I shouted as he smiled and ran to me. Stella was napping in my arms so I couldn't give him a full hug. But I was thrilled my baby boy had run straight toward me. Used to his nonchalance toward affection, I'd been worried he'd lose interest in me during my hospital stay.

Turns out I wasn't entirely off the mark.

He reached his arms up in the international toddler gesture for "pick me up."

"I'm sorry, honey, but I can't pick you up. I'm holding your new baby."

Mika dashed over and hoisted our son onto the bed. Leo reached his arms out again, this time to Stella. Ah, I understood then what he had meant. He'd actually been giving the international symbol for "Mom, you're old news, let me hold the baby."

No way was I letting my rambunctious 21-month-old

---

[16] No, we did not name her after the beer Stella Artois, but thanks for being the fiftieth person to ask. As much as I enjoy Stella Artois, I prefer Guinness. But I really prefer champagne to beer. Since I won't name my daughter Guinness or Moet & Chandon, it's safe to assume her name was not alcohol-inspired.

hold his newborn sister, but I let him pat her head. He gave her a kiss, then poked her nose and made a "boop" noise, the same noise I make when he pokes my nose. He was surprisingly calm and gentle.

"Doudou! Doudou de Maman!" he declared.

How sweet! He had called Stella "Mommy's *doudou*" as if she were my cuddly little lovey. Well, she kind of was.

"Get this," Mika said. "Did you know that our daughter's birthday is Star Wars Day?"

"No, I didn't. What's Star Wars Day?"

"May the 4th be with you."

"Ha! That's awesome."

"And it's Audrey Hepburn's birthday, too," he said.

How perfect. My beautiful daughter shared a birthday with one of the world's classiest ladies as well as a movie with maybe the world's geekiest fan base. My future supermodel scientist had the whole world in front of her.

"Maman!" Leo said, pointing to me. "Papa," he said, pointing to Mika. "Bébé," he added, pointing to Stella.

And I had my perfect little family in front of me.

See how it all began in *Confessions of a Paris Party Girl!*

A Note from Vicki Lesage

Dear Reader,

Thanks for reading *Confessions of a Paris Potty Trainer*! I wrote it while I was on bed rest after going into preterm labor when I was pregnant with my daughter. Writing really helped me through those long months (which felt more like *years*). Now, every time I see my daughter running around and laughing—inevitably causing trouble with her older brother—I'm so grateful at how everything worked out. Thank you for being a part of my journey.

I hope you enjoyed the book! If so, I'd love it if you left a review on Amazon.com. For every review—even just a few sentences—I receive a cupcake. OK, not really. But customer reviews encourage readers to try out new books, which is arguably better. Depending on the flavor of cupcake.

If you'd like to see how my adventure in Paris began, check out *Confessions of a Paris Party Girl!* I also post updates on what I'm doing these days on my website and in my newsletters. And I love hearing from readers, so feel free to drop me a line at vicki@vickilesage.com.

Thanks for reading!

À bientôt,
Vicki

P.S. Read on for a sneak peek of *Confessions of a Paris Party Girl…*

CATCH UP ON
Confessions

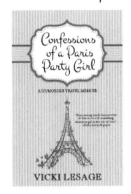

Confessions of a Paris Party Girl

A HUMOROUS TRAVEL MEMOIR

VICKI LESAGE

press

Sarah's Coming To Town

"I BOOKED MY FLIGHT!" my step-sister Sarah announced over the crackling long-distance line.

"Awesome! I can't wait to show you around."

Though I had only been living in the city a short while, I was getting used to my new life, picking up baguettes and passing centuries-old architecture. I don't think I'll ever tire of them—Paris is way too awesome for that—but you do reach a point where you go about your daily business without really noticing them. This became most evident on Sarah's visit.

Since my parents were divorced, Stephen and I spent our summers with our dad and step-family in sunny Florida. The five-bedroom house was bursting at the seams with our modern-day Brady Bunch of three boys and three girls. We got into all sorts of trouble in very short amounts of time.

Whenever one of the five other kids wanted something (ice cream, movie rentals, a new bike), they would send me to ask Dad because they said I was his favorite. Maybe I was, or maybe they just wanted me to do their dirty work for them. But in the end, it nearly always worked.

One summer when I was about 12, Sarah, 6 months my junior, decided we needed a pool. It took a little more asking than a trip to the ice cream parlor. "Pleeeeeeeeease, Dad? We promise to never ask for anything else ever again and to obey all your rules."

"Here's a rule: just play in the sprinklers. It's the same thing."

Was he kidding? I was going to have to approach this from a different angle. As a thermodynamics engineer, my dad would respond best to straightforward logic. "Dad, look. If you get a pool, we'll swim in it every day and we won't need any other entertainment. But if you don't get us a pool then we'll need to rent movies and go to the arcade and buy lots of other new stuff to be happy. If you think about it, we're actually saving you money."

"I'm not sure your math works out on that, honey."

I looked back at the gang and shrugged my shoulders. Sarah made a motion with her hand, laying it flat and lifting it up high. Huh? Oh... I get it. "We'd settle for an above-ground pool. It's much cheaper."

"Above-ground pool? That's a bit redneck but you're right it's a lot cheaper. I'll think about it." That was as good as a yes in my previous experience.

After the pool was installed and filled (which takes way longer than a kid has patience for), we hopped in and didn't get out all weekend except for bathroom breaks and sunscreen re-applications. At least, I hope everyone got out for bathroom breaks.

On Monday morning, when our parents left for work, they gave us stern instructions.

"Be careful around the pool and wear sunscreen," my step-mom, Marsha, said.

"And no jumping off the roof into the pool," Dad added.

"Jumping off the roof into the pool? We hadn't thought of that, but now that you mention it, what a great idea!" we collectively thought.

We nodded, our most angelic smiles convincingly plastered to our faces. Not five minutes after our parents were out the door, we were in our swimsuits in the backyard, eyeing the roof.

"I guess a ladder is the best way up," Sarah offered. My older step-brother, Isaac, nodded his agreement.

Propping a ladder against the side of the house would be conspicuous, but then again, so was running off the roof into the pool.

"Are you sure the pool is deep enough?" I asked.

"Yeah, yeah," Sarah assured me.

It didn't seem deep enough to me, but maybe an above-ground pool didn't need to be as deep? We all seemed to be thinking the same thing as we paused in thought. Then Sarah snapped us out of it. "There's only one way to find out!"

One by one, we climbed the ladder. From that angle, the pool sure did seem far away. But once we were up there, no one wanted to chicken out.

"We need a running start in order to clear the edge of the pool," Sarah proclaimed.

I was getting woozier by the minute. I'm not afraid of heights, but I am afraid of knocking my teeth out. Ever since I fell off a row of bleachers and knocked out my front teeth two years earlier (don't worry, they've since been replaced), I'd been afraid of heights-as-tall-as-bleachers. Which was coincidentally the same height as jumping from the roof of a one-story house into a pool.

Without giving it much more thought, Sarah ran off the roof and splashed into the pool. When she surfaced without incident, it gave Isaac, Stephen, and my younger step-brother, Jake, all the encouragement they needed to plunge in after her.

Rebecca, my older step-sister, was not one to be left out and jumped in next.

I was now alone on the roof, my bare feet gripping the gritty roof tiles, my pale, freckly skin exposed for all the neighborhood to see. I had to do it. I couldn't turn back now unless I wanted to be teased the rest of the summer. And I had to do it quickly before I got busted.

Well, you can always get new teeth. I should know.

So I jumped. As I came back up through the water, I was astounded I hadn't broken anything, but I ran my finger across my teeth to be sure. Yep, all there.

Everyone took turns jumping off the roof the rest of the day. Since I'd done it once, I avoided their ridicule and instead passed the day splashing around and dreaming of suntanned skin.

Over dinner that night, Dad asked if we'd behaved. Why do parents ask questions like that? We're never going to answer no.

"You all had fun in the pool today?" It sounded simple enough, but his tone implied it was a test. Everyone looked at me to respond.

"Yep! Thanks for getting it for us."

"No one jumped off the roof?"

"Ha, heh, um, no!" I stammered. How much did he know?

"Then do you have any idea how all that gravel got in there? The gravel that's the exact color of the roof tiles?"

I couldn't hold my innocent expression much longer. "Um, maybe because of the sand? We are in Florida after all," I tried.

"That's not what the neighbor said."

My stomach dropped. He knew! My face was surely red. Everyone else stared down at their plates. How would I get us out of this?

"Which neighbor? The crazy redneck next door?" I'd throw that guy under the bus if it would save us.

"No, Ron across the street." He was triumphant. He knew he had us. "You guys had one rule and you broke it. I bet you were out on the roof ten minutes after we left." More like five minutes, we simultaneously thought. We knew not to look at one another or else we'd burst out laughing.

"Now, I can't take the pool away but you're all grounded for two weeks. And no more jumping off the roof. If you do, I'll drain that pool faster than you can swim out of it!"

∽∾

The minute Sarah got off the plane in Paris, we hit the ground running and made the tour of my usual bar circuit. Jetlagged and tipsy, she rattled off all the places she couldn't wait to visit the next day. While I'd seen most of the sites myself, I didn't mind showing her around because you can't ever get too much of Paris.

Halfway through our pub crawl, we passed Notre Dame. I was hurrying because we were late for meeting Lisa and Katrina for karaoke, and Sarah was lagging behind.

"It's just a bit further up this way, Sarah. C'mon!" If we didn't hurry, the karaoke line would be super long and we'd have to sit through a bunch of crappy songs before belting out our own crappy renditions.

"Chill! Can't a girl enjoy the view in peace?" She paused and let out an audible gasp. "Oh my God. Is that Notre DAME? You walk past Notre Dame on your way to the bars? How cool!"

I stopped. I hadn't thought about it but she was right. That was really cool.

"I'm tipsy in front of Notre Dame. Isn't that, like, sacrilegious? But, like, wouldn't it be worse if I walked past without stopping?"

Good point. I suppose karaoke could wait while we had a look-see at the cathedral.

We crossed the pedestrian bridge to get a closer view. It truly is a magnificent church. So ancient, so detailed, so beautiful. No matter how many images you've seen in books or movies, nothing prepares you for how amazing it is up close.

"Buuuuurp." Ahem. Perhaps I shouldn't have finished my last drink so quickly. I silently apologized to God for being so rude before shuffling Sarah along. "We'll come back tomorrow. It will be much better and much less blasphemous. We'll wake up bright and early and conquer the city."

৵৵

The next day, we woke up groggy and late, but still covered quite a bit of town. We caught up on gossip and reminisced about old times while winding our way through medieval cobblestone streets.

I felt proud to be showing "my city" to a guest and happy to be sharing it with my step-sister. Nothing makes you feel like a local faster. Maybe two weeks ago I was a clueless American making rookie mistakes, but now my step-sister was the rookie and I was the one who knew what was going on.

From the way I'd walk off the Métro before it came to a complete stop (livin' on the edge, baby!) to knowing the owner of the restaurants we dined at, big city living was already second nature.

One of my favorite places, aside from my slew of regular bars, was Refuge des Fondus. Popular with tourists, this rowdy fondue restaurant is usually half-occupied by locals as well. It's hard to say what I like most about the restaurant—from the graffitied walls to climbing over the communal table to sit on the side against the wall—its grungy ambience is a sharp contrast to typical Parisian eateries. It's not unusual for the entire restaurant to sing "Happy Birthday" to a fellow patron, making the rounds in several different languages. And on top of that I get a huge pot of melted cheese? Count me in!

I lied when I said I didn't know what I liked most about the place. Their gimmick is that you drink wine out of baby bottles and this is what stole my heart. It's a guaranteed hit with out-of-town guests, who wear out their camera batteries in various poses with the baby bottles.

In my vast experience, I've discovered that the perfect amount to consume is four baby bottles. Three baby bottles equal one full bottle of wine, so four of the little guys is just the right amount to get you singing "Feliz Compleaños" to the group of Spaniards across the restaurant while still being able to find your way home at the end of the night.

Believe it or not, the owners of this establishment actually like me. I guess because for once, being a tipsy singing girl is the norm. When arriving for a reservation, we always greet each other with la bise, the French custom of kissing friends on each cheek. As the long line of hungry patrons outside stares in envy, I can't help but feel cool at being immediately ushered to my table. That might be due more to having a reservation (the restaurant only holds 40 people) than them liking me, but then again they do have my picture posted on the wall. Tough call.

On around my 40th visit, I graffitied my own message on the wall, "La Reine de Fondue." Fondue Queen. Self-proclaimed French royalty. By my 60th visit, I made my own punch card. Surprisingly, they honored it—stamping it each time I came and offering me a free digestif when I had filled all ten slots. After my 100th visit, I stopped counting how many times I'd been there. I'm sure I could get a rough estimate by reading my cholesterol chart.

❧

When Sarah, Lisa, Katrina, and I arrived at the restaurant on the last evening of Sarah's trip, the staff gave us the friendliest of welcomes and immediately brought over the wine. By the time we slammed our 4th baby bottles down on the table, the restaurant had heard the greatest hits from "The Little Mermaid" as well as the crowd-pleasing sing-a-long, "Sweet Caroline." Bellies full of cheese and wine, vocal cords overused and raspy, the evening had been a wild success.

Out of all the places I'd taken her to, the fondue restaurant was the highlight of Sarah's trip. We were crazy kids again, in a different setting. The girl who had once been scared to jump into the pool had now crossed an ocean and was doing just fine.

Find out what happens next… pick up *Confessions of a Paris Party Girl* today!

About the Author

Vicki lived in Paris for many years, where she met her husband, Mika, and had two kids, Leo and Stella. After admitting that a one-bedroom Parisian apartment was too small for the four of them, they moved to Vicki's hometown of St. Louis and have been enjoying the extra space ever since. Vicki still misses croissants and baguettes and stinky cheese, though.

Catch up on the latest from Vicki:
Website: VickiLesage.com
Newsletter: https://bit.ly/lesage-news
Facebook: https://www.facebook.com/vickilesagewriter

And you can always drop Vicki a line at vicki@vickilesage.com. Mail from readers is the best part of her day. Unless the kids actually let her sleep in for once, in which case she'll get to your email momentarily!

Acknowledgements

Many thanks to Ellen Meyer, a.k.a. Mom, who reminded me of anecdotes for this book that my "baby brain" had forgotten. Thanks, too, for editing, re-editing, and formatting the whole thing, which I know isn't the most fun way for a new grandma to spend her time, but greatly improved the book.

Huge thanks to Marie Vareille, fellow author and meticulous editor, who provided invaluable feedback and a French perspective. I'd also like to thank Clara Vidal who created the cover for my first book, *Confessions of a Paris Party Girl*, providing the perfect template for this sequel (and saving me a ton of time). Thanks to Damien Croisot for polishing up my author photo. If only he could make my skin look that good in real life!

I want to thank my husband, Mickaël Lesage, for his love, support, and humor. Every day of my life is better with him in it and every page of this book is better because of him. He took on Daddy Duty like a champ during my bed rest, which allowed me to not only write this book, but gestate our baby many weeks past the preterm labor incident. And I'd like to thank Leonardo and Stella, my beautiful children who, in addition to giving me a reason to smile every day, gave me plenty of material for this book.

Made in the USA
Middletown, DE
12 April 2021